Garden Farming

Hugh Lanham

THE CROWOOD PRESS

First published in 2010 by
The Crowood Press Ltd
Ramsbury, Marlborough
Wiltshire SN8 2HR

www.crowood.com

British Library Cataloguing-in-Publication Data
A catalogue record for this book is available from the British Library.

ISBN 978 1 84797 166 1

Acknowledgements
Although I write this book as if I do it all, my wife Claire does more than her fair share. I therefore dedicate it to her. My thanks go also to my daughter Emily, whose diligent proof reading helped so much.

Designed and typeset by Focus Publishing,
11a St Botolph's Road, Sevenoaks, Kent TN13 3AJ

Printed and bound in Singapore by Craft Print International Ltd

Contents

CHAPTER 1

Introducing
the Idea

People take up domestic food production for a lot of different reasons. For me, one motivation is trying to be the farmer that I always wanted to be 'when I am grown up', and I think I get as much satisfaction from both growing things and working with livestock on a small scale, as if my dream had been realized. Indeed, farming is probably overrated anyway: too much time spent stuck in a tractor cab and, for livestock farmers, too much of a tie – imagine being committed to a hundred cows needing to be milked three times a day.

Garden farming must not, for me, become peasant farming. I want it to enhance my existing way of life. I don't want to give up my job: it isn't perfect, but it does give me mental stimulation and a decent income, and I simply don't want to give it up just for the rather earthy satisfaction of mucking out the pigs.

The second motivation for garden farming is my stomach. We enjoy very good quality food. We have meat from rarer breeds of livestock, and choose our vegetable and fruit varieties for flavour rather than keeping quality. I cannot stress enough the difference in flavour between some of our produce and the food that you can buy. We also have a much better idea of what goes into our food.

I am not one to get too hung up on pesticides, GM crops and additives, but many people, perhaps wiser than I, are concerned. Indeed, modern farming has been one of the most spectacular industries the world has ever seen in terms of efficiency. Commercial food is amazingly cheap and reliable, but we have no need to replicate that: we are after something a little different.

Our approach is always to minimize the use of chemicals and additives, and to be as natural as possible. Nature's way, after all, is really quite striking, in that green vegetation is used as food by animals, which pay for it with nothing more than excrement and their own carcasses when their lives are done. Other 'higher' animals, the carnivores and omnivores, pay the same price for eating the herbivores (or their eggs and milk). This is a decent deal if ever there was one, but as humans we seem increasingly reluctant to subscribe to it! As a boy I recall that for many, the Sunday routine included burying the contents of the lavatory bucket, and many a good vegetable patch thrived on that – but now it all gets

Supper picked.

flushed away! Indeed, it has become a problem called pollution. And carcasses now have to be burnt: this is progress!

The great virtue of this cycle is that it has survived for many tens of thousands of years with only minor change. Modern sophisticated techniques are not so well tested. In the garden farm we look to that cycle as a mainstay of our practice. The soil grows food; we share the food with the animals, which produce manure; we feed the soil with their manure, and eat the animals. Personally I think there is no good reason for not feeding the soil with our own manure too, but some might argue there is a

disease risk. OK, so we let this one go, and sensitivities will be respected.

Garden farming is hardly new: it is a development of what allotment keepers have been doing for scores of years. We are aiming to produce as much as possible of our own food from whatever land we have access to. The traditional allotment of 10 rods – about 250sq m (300sq yd) – became standardized at that size, not just because of a bureaucratic whim but because it was big enough to produce most of the vegetables that a family would eat, and because it was a manageable size of plot for a working family. The greatest growth in allotment holding was during

The cycle in action on a very natural scale.

World War II, and by about 1942 it reached its peak with some 1,500,000 allotments in cultivation, in addition to back gardens. This means that a significant proportion of the population was eating home-grown vegetables; indeed a significant proportion of the nation's food was being produced by hand on a small scale. Today, interest in allotments and vegetable gardens (although rather smaller in general) is showing signs of recovery. Long may it last.

From the early days allotment holders have had the right to keep hens and rabbits, too. Many councils are now keen to suppress this right, as livestock bring noise and vermin often quite close to houses – but the right is certainly still there, and this allows for the production of some meat and, of course, eggs in addition to the fruit and vegetables. The pig was never really an allotment animal, but many a small cottage had a pigsty, and for centuries people were able to make a very significant contribution to their family's diet by killing a couple of pigs every year.

For all the legislative difficulties now faced by pig keepers it is still possible, and very rewarding, to produce pork, bacon and sausages from the bottom of the garden, although these days it is necessary to first check your deeds and with the neighbours, as it is no longer 'normal' behaviour.

From our own garden we do not claim, nor do we want to claim, that we are self-sufficient or truly organic, but we do produce a great deal of very good food. In accepting that all our food cannot be produced at home we need to set our priorities and identify which types of food we most want to produce for ourselves. The greatest challenges are in meat production, but also the greatest rewards, since meat is expensive and where the majority of scares are focused.

Interest in organic ideas and techniques has had a major impact on our approach to food and what goes into its production. Essentially, organic thinking has concentrated minds on natural and generally old-fashioned methods of food production. This is very laudable and, subject to a few reservations, I am certain that following the organic pathway produces great food with the lowest possible risks. The biggest reservation, which is perhaps worth a mention, relates to medicines. If your animal is sick and suffering, should you stick to organic principals, or use whatever is necessary to heal it? I leave readers to decide for themselves.

We also have to fit the ambition for healthy and good food into a tight working timetable, and if we are too strict about production techniques we may fail to produce much food at all, which sends us straight back to the supermarket. However, by compromising on a few things we should be able to achieve ends that are much more satisfactory than supermarket produce, even if they are not perfectly organic.

MY PREJUDICES

Below is the list of my own priorities and choices. They are personal prejudices at least as much as facts. Readers will doubtless wish to choose different ones for themselves, but planning to protect yourself from those that concern you most is very important. You will not achieve everything.

Food flavour: We have all heard the complaint that food from supermarkets today does not taste as good as did food in the past. Grow your own in well kept soil and try it. I think the complaint is well founded; most crops need to be eaten within hours of picking to retain the very best taste, and they can rarely be that fresh from the shops.

Despite the appearance of loaded supermarket shelves there really is very little choice both in terms of types of food

and especially in terms of varieties. Some of the very best flavours are simply not available in any shops because, maybe, the skins are too delicate to allow for mass handling techniques or they don't all ripen predictably for the supermarket buyer. As a result growing the maximum possible proportion of these things is a prime motivation.

Food scares: The last few years have seen more than enough food scares: salmonella, BSE, e-coli, spray residues and a build-up of resistance to antibiotics as a result of adding it to the ration, to name but a few. As I have said, the science of food production is extremely sophisticated (but distrusted), and it is difficult, if not impossible for most of us to be well enough informed to assess what is, and what is not, safe. We therefore take a cautious route.

Sprays and artificial fertilizers: Vegetables and salad crops are grown commercially both in fields and in greenhouses. What is common to both techniques is that sprays and artificial fertilizers are used extensively. There may, or may not, be risk attached to this (I think there is). Some crops are never even planted in earth, but are grown in a fertilizer solution 'hydroponically'; I do not know whether to worry about that or not. It certainly does not feel exactly natural, and my feeling is that flavour generally does suffer from these techniques.

Beef and milk: Cattle have had BSE, and that worries me; so if I'm going to eat beef or drink milk I'd rather know that the herd was clean and that it had eaten grass. Even then I know that something will be fed to it in addition to the grass – some type of protein out of a bag, and I'd like to know what that protein is (but no one will tell me). Probably I'd be happy if I knew it was lucerne. I don't know enough about genetically modified soya to form an opinion, so I'd rather it wasn't from that. What about fishmeal? Again, I don't know. Personally on this scale I don't consider cattle, and concentrate on producing other types of meat. If you have grazing to spare this may be different, but gardens are not usually that big.

Lamb production: My first instinct is that lamb should be safe, as mostly lambs eat grass. Scrapie, though, appeared in sheep long before BSE in cattle and is very similar. Also, I know it doesn't actually glow in the dark, but some farms received such high doses of radiation from Chernobyl that their lamb could not be sold. I'm not happy that the limits are set so accurately that a farm which marginally passes the radiation test produces safe lamb.

Producing pork: Pork used not to worry me as I felt that pigs were designed to eat, amongst other things, animal waste. Surely they are then likely not to allow diseases to cross from one species to another? Maybe. The thing that worries me now is that the sheer intensity of commercial production cannot possibly be healthy and indeed the high additive levels in pig feeds are, at least in part, designed to overcome this basic risk. I have to say, as well, that there is an issue about just how far you can reasonably abuse animals, and the way a lot of pigs are kept leaves me uncomfortable about eating pork. There are now large outdoor herds of pigs replacing some of the indoor ones. This may be a good thing, but when you see animals cold, wet and muddy, or at the other extreme getting sunburnt, you can

worry about this, too; it is not really all that 'natural' as there is very little nutrition for pigs from the soil if kept so intensively. Anyway, pigs are such a great joy to keep at home that this has to be the best of all, especially when you can control their diet.

Poultry keeping: Poultry of all types have been fed on animal waste for a century with no apparent ill effects from that. They, like most pigs, are kept too intensively for my liking, but my own prejudice is that for birds, this is less of an issue than for mammals. Eggs are probably also a very good way of feeding humans with minimal risk of disease transfer, and I therefore worry less here than in other areas. However, popular prejudice is not at all happy with poultry-keeping practice, and again, readers must decide for themselves. One should also not overlook salmonella, but the risk here applies to all types of production, including pens in your garden. At home, though, you can keep nest boxes clean and discard dirty eggs rather than wash them, and perhaps where you are exposed to the same bacteria all the time you build up your resistance.

Over-intensive accommodation of livestock: As I write this, fears of a bird flu epidemic and of its possible transfer to humans underlines, if nothing else, the issue concerning the over-intensive accommodation of livestock. It seems that the source of the disease is almost certainly very intensive caging practices in the Far East.

Animal welfare: On the subject of animal welfare, opinions vary widely. For me, on a graph of human awfulness that includes holocaust and war, animal welfare hardly

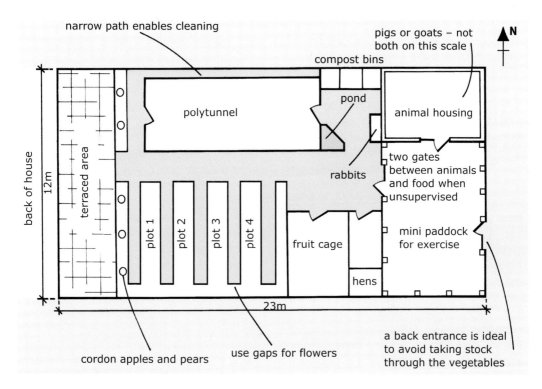

narrow path enables cleaning

pigs or goats – not
both on this scale

compost bins

N

polytunnel

pond

animal housing

back of house

12m

terraced area

rabbits

two gates
between animals
and food when
unsupervised

plot 1

plot 2

plot 3

plot 4

fruit cage

mini paddock
for exercise

hens

23m

cordon apples and pears

use gaps for flowers

a back entrance is ideal
to avoid taking stock
through the vegetables

A compact garden farm layout.

leaves the horizontal axis. It is, I believe, seriously distorted in the modern mind by childhood exposure to anthropomorphic images of Peter Rabbit and Disney. Nevertheless, faced with bad examples of modern abattoir techniques or bad intensive pig farms, we must all feel at least uncomfortable, if not disgusted. Let us not pretend that we grow animals otherwise than to kill them, but producing your own food allows you control of all parts of the process and enables you to concentrate on decent husbandry and slaughter.

OUR OWN APPROACH

We produce most of our own vegetables and a good amount for the animals. We would call the vegetables organic except that we occasionally use slug pellets, and seeds that have been treated with seed dressings. If we do use pellets we cover the beds to keep the birds away from them, and never use them once the frogs and toads have come out of hibernation; these friends do more than anything else to control our slugs.

If we were strictly organic we would use beer traps for slugs and spend a lot of time picking off invaders by hand; however, we do not have that time. Nevertheless, we strongly subscribe to the root of organic theory that soil condition and feeding is very important indeed. It helps to make the plants stronger and to look after themselves better in the fight with pests, diseases and also, particularly in some recent summers here in the east of England, with drought. When pests or diseases become too great a problem we grow something else. I would be lying if I said we never failed with anything, but we certainly produce enough to eat well.

Muck for the soil is very important, and we produce all that we need ourselves (if anything, getting rid of it can be our problem). If we were to run short of it we would buy some in and not worry at all about whether it was organic or not. Maybe we should, but having muck is more important to me than being too fussy.

We try to save some of our own seed because it is very satisfying to do so. There is no way, though, that I would not buy the seeds I wanted just because of seed dressing. It is much more important to get things growing well than for them to fail, because that failure again takes me back to the supermarket whose produce carries some, if not all, of the risks that we have already identified.

For meat production we look first to rabbits and then to pigs or ducks. We have kept a lot of other things, but only when we have had the time. It is possible to produce two or three rabbits per week at a little over 1kg (2.2lb) each – and more, if you want them – without too much difficulty from fewer than ten hutches. Two pigs reared to about pork weight (or a little more) once or twice every year will each yield 50kg (110lb) of meat each.

Ducks are becoming increasingly important, in our thinking. They eat nearly anything (especially muscovy ducks), and there are fewer legal problems with waste food with them than there are for pigs. Otherwise our poultry is kept mainly for egg production – though hatching a clutch of chicks every spring to keep the laying flock young gives a few good chicken meals both from surplus cockerels and from the older birds that we are replacing.

There is no doubt that a freezer is important to us to spread out the gluts.

We buy good quality additive-free feed wherever possible, but most of it is not strictly organic; for example, we buy a little grain from a local farmer to be able to throw a handful or two to the hens every day. He is not organic, but this grain was going to enter the food chain somewhere, either directly for human feed (perhaps as bread) or via animals. Via animals feels safer to me.

Straw for the animals when it is bought in can rarely be organic so we put up with what we can get. Hay bought in is unlikely to have been subjected to much chemical attack except an occasional application of nitrogen. Herbicides can creep in, however, and the best solution is to ask the farmer when, if ever, they were last used.

Egg production on the domestic scale is relatively easy; most of the work is in tracking down additive-free feeds of sufficient protein content. Again it is easy to buy ordinary chicken pellets, but then what advantage do your eggs have over the shop ones? Not much, I suspect. Subject to legal restrictions, mostly relating to pigs, food scraps can be an important source of food, especially protein for poultry. The problem is that as the number of mouths requiring food increases, the amount of food that each receives from scraps decreases. Scraps are also by their nature irregular and some bought-in food must always be available.

QUALITY OF LIFE

For us, some vegetable growing is relatively easy to fit into a normal working week. There is little pressure, and most of the time the next job will wait until the

The author's vegetable garden with pigs beyond and, to the right, apple trees in a small paddock used for poultry. Note the guards around the good trees for when sheep graze there.

following weekend. This enables us to enjoy being outside, gardening at our own pace and listening to the birds sing. They do not all sing too sweetly, it must be said, but I like to listen even to the magpies.

As soon as we move into livestock the commitments increase. There is normally a requirement to feed them at least twice a day, and to muck them out frequently as well as the weekend jobs. As the livestock get larger, unless you have fields to graze them in, so the commitment increases. This goes on to the extent that the ostrich family which I shall cover, briefly, can require a wild animal licence which in some areas still demands all day attendance.

Although livestock is a commitment (despite the suggestions I shall offer for reducing it to a minimum), there is an immense pleasure in getting up just those few minutes earlier in order to get outside and feed them all before going off to the office. Not only is communing with livestock always pleasurable, there is also an involvement with the elements, which, despite huge viewing figures for weather forecasts, are becoming increasingly excluded from our experience as we drive from warm home to warm office in warm car.

For the summer evenings and at weekends there will be a bit more time to enjoy the outdoors. Take time to absorb it. If you can, use a spade, not a rotovator. It will avoid spoiling the neighbour's Sunday afternoon snooze as well as giving you much more chance to involve yourself with the nature around. Digging can even make some useful contribution to getting fit, although, sadly, I find not enough; other exercise still needs to be taken. If you have any grass left in your garden once the 'farming' has taken over you will need a lawn mower – but think about grazing creatures first and use the mower as little as possible. Mainly it should be used to maintain the quality of your grass, in that 'topping off' the bits not eaten by the animals maintains its condition. Rabbits in arks, geese and tethered goats may all be used to graze, and we shall come to them later in this book.

The harvest is always rewarding, but there is a benefit that you don't really plan for, in that if you shop for your food you buy a reasonable amount for a meal, whereas the garden farmer uses what he has produced and enjoys both tiny amounts and gluts. Thus there is the double treat, firstly of the first few fresh asparagus spears of the season, and then a week later the sheer indulgence of having to eat much more than you would have bought!

Do not forget the visual aspects, either: I am writing this section early in October and the house is decorated with bowls of various squashes, vases of flowers and bunches of herbs drying, as too are the globe artichoke heads that were too small to eat and which we shall use for Christmas decorations. The vegetable store and freezer are full, and that looks good as well as giving a wonderful sense of primitive security.

HOLIDAYS

I know that the pleasure we have from our plot is so great that we never wish to leave the place, but if there is anything more contrived to make growing things difficult it is that the schools give holidays at crucial moments in the gardening calendar. Good if you are a teacher, of course, but otherwise taking the children away for a break can cause problems. Particular conflicts are Easter, when the potatoes need planting, and the summer holidays, where if you are away too long you simply miss the majority of the crops you spent the rest of the year growing (also watering can be pretty crucial then).

The basic solution is, I am afraid, to keep holidays short; we work on the little and often principal. At Easter, once all the spring sowing is done, potatoes planted and soil brought under control, there should be a bit of the holiday left. In the summer, take an early week after picking everything aggressively and watering copiously. Come back and do the same again before another break if you want one. One hot summer we took a fortnight's break and lost all our beans; since we normally fill several drawers of the freezer with these, that was too upsetting a loss.

Christmas holidays spent in the sun or skiing are both popular and available now. In winter there is very little you can do in the garden, certainly nothing that cannot be delayed a week or two, so indulge yourself then.

The other problem is the livestock, and if you cannot find a neighbour who can cast an eye over things at least once a day when you are away, then it may not be possible to keep them. As we get to the animal sections I have tried to start with those that are least demanding of labour, and have graduated to the large milking animals, which are another level of tie altogether. The first animal, the rabbit, can be kept using commercial equipment that will give feed in hoppers, water from watering systems and cages where the muck drops straight out. Poultry can certainly be treated in a similar way – although they are quite capable of filling the hoppers with straw so that they starve themselves; however, certainly for a week they could be visited only once a day and be expected to survive. 'Do keep the eggs' is often quite a good motivator.

Success with holidays is a matter of planning. We use a large wall chart and mark our holidays on first. Then we mark the weeks when it would be convenient to harvest and, more particularly, kill live-stock that is to be fattened (usually just before we go away). Book the butcher! Knowing the rearing time, we then work out when to buy the weaners, chicks or whatever to suit the plan. We do see this process as fundamental to what we do, and holidays as very important indeed.

Having reduced the livestock to the minimum when we go away, we still have to plan for some care from friends and make sure that there will be plenty of food and clear instructions available for the good neighbour to use.

CHAPTER 2

Vegetable Growing Systems and Techniques

MUCK

There may be no answer to the question 'which came first, the chicken or the egg', but in the cycle of food production of plants, livestock and muck, always start with the muck. Even if you subscribe to the view that being purely organic is too extreme for you either philosophically or practically, manure and compost have to be central. As a supplier of nutrients for the soil, good muck is very beneficial; as a soil conditioner it is fabulously useful, especially for regulating moisture. Yes, it is true, not only does muck help with dry soils very considerably, it can also help keep very wet soil open and so avoid waterlogging.

There are few 'free lunches' even for the gardener. If the soil is not looked after and fed well, output will at best be poor. Like a board game or puzzle, this is the point marked 'Start here'. Normally muck is divided into manure and compost, but for us the distinction often gets blurred.

Manure

Manure tends to be extracted from the pile of stable rubbish that accumulates wher-ever livestock is kept on straw. Perversely, the worse the husbandry the better the muck. Three things make for a 'good drop' produced on the casual heap system:

- large amounts of dung and not too much straw;
- enough urine to make it moist when it goes on the pile;
- enough time for it to fester and break down.

Keeping any stock in conditions that produce muck like this is unacceptable, and so most heaps tend to have far too great a proportion of straw. As the straw breaks down, it steals nitrogen from the active ingredients (the droppings and urine), leaving a good soil conditioner but with little nourishing effect.

There are techniques used for control-ling and improving the rotting process of various manures, many of which can be very effective. Given that we care about what the garden looks like but have time constraints, our ambitions are to find quick, tidy techniques that cope with the wide variety of sources of material to rot.

The rabbits, goats and other stock all give dry, strawy manure that usually

The author's vegetable garden.

contains some juicy bits of muck, a lot of straw and some spilt food. When we clean them out this gets barrowed either to the hen yard and tipped as deep litter (*see* Chapter 11), or given to the pigs in their outside runs. Neither hens nor pigs are offended by rejects from other stock or by the food that their digestions only partly processed, and both will work through this used straw, getting benefit from it. Also a great deal of the stuff that would normally go on a compost bin can be thrown in for various livestock to sort through, and anything not eaten directly ends up in the mix.

In time you start sorting your rubbish in the following way:

■ clean green food and washed roots (not potatoes) for the rabbits;
■ weeds and rotten vegetables for the ducks and pigs;
■ household scraps to poultry.

There are some limitations, such as the fact that nothing gets through large quantities of grass mowings in the height of the season (once they start rotting, which they do after only a few hours in hot weather, they must be cleared away) and rhubarb leaves (which nothing eats).

When the straw has to be cleared from outside straw yards and daily from the larger animals, we clear it to bins. In the end it all ends up here.

The Compost Bin

Everything that doesn't go through an animal, and everything that has, comes here, to the compost bin, to rot. The object is to produce an environment for decomposition by aerobic bacteria. The primary requirements are air, moisture, insulation and something for these bacteria to eat (the material for rotting). A good bin should get quite hot (around 45° C or more), and this will kill most weed seeds and a lot of diseases.

The standard compost bin is built from planks of wood and is a 1m (3ft) cube in size. Generally they are built in pairs. In order for the material to be handled the front of the bins must be removable. Many books have drawn the hammer and nail pictures and most gardeners will be familiar with them. One point to stress, because we sometimes get it wrong, is the need to organize adequate ventilation into the bin at the bottom with rows of bricks, old pipes or whatever is available. If your rots get too black and nasty, try a drain-pipe down the middle as well while building the heap – take it out to get air through when you have finished building it.

Decent planks for this type of bin are becoming increasingly expensive, so don't be shy of trying other materials such as concrete, brick or composite boards, as long as they provide good insulation. Remember when using wood preservative that it is designed to prevent rotting, and that compost heaps are designed to encourage it; at least wait until the stuff is well and truly dry.

The compost bins; here the three-bin system.

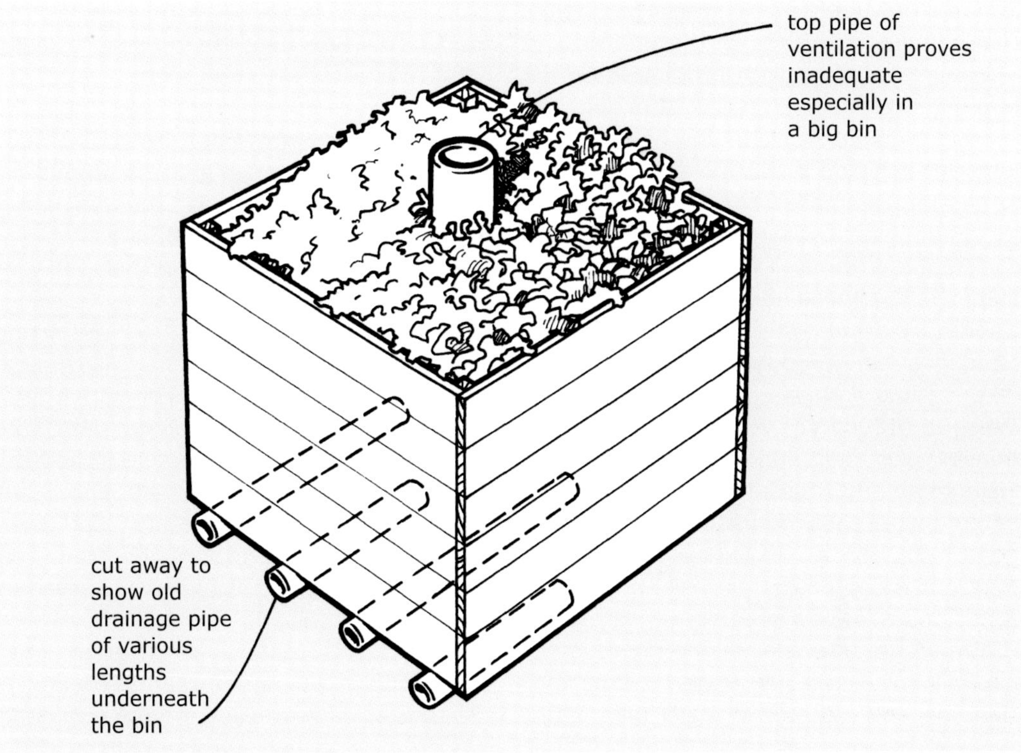

top pipe of
ventilation proves
inadequate
especially in
a big bin

cut away to
show old
drainage pipe
of various
lengths
underneath
the bin

Ventilation of the bin.

Any organic material can be used for making compost. I remember attending a lecture by the late, great, W. E. Shewell-Cooper who opened his talk by booming to the back of the hall (and probably well beyond) in a voice loud enough to wake the dead 'Anything that has lived can live again in a compost heap'. His examples even extended to his old tweed jacket, but times move on and I doubt if I have any that are not riddled with synthetic fibres, which wouldn't rot. Generally, despite his counsel, I would not try to rot anything woody (let alone wooden) to avoid lumps in the final product.

In practice the word 'heap' is a misnomer: you will never get decent results from a heap, and a bin should always be constructed. Good bins need adequate moisture and their composition should also bear that in mind. To get sufficient moisture into the bins in a dry period, lawn mowings and other greenstuffs are very valuable. Their availability should trigger the filling of a bin. Try to get a bin filled over as few weeks as possible for fastest rotting. We produce our premium brew every spring. When the grass is growing strongly we fill a complete bin in only a couple of weekends with grass cuttings in thin layers alternated with the contents of the animal pens and yards. This brew gives our fastest and hottest rot and is, not surprisingly, our best muck.

After a couple of months (more in the winter) the bin cools down and must be turned. This sets off a small secondary heating up and finishes off the job. Here is where I take issue with other authorities who build their bins in pairs. After the first heating the volume in the bin has reduced to about half and it therefore needs to be turned into a smaller bin, or alternatively two bins need to be turned into one. My preference is for two large bins of about 1.3m (4.3ft) in all dimensions, and two standard bins of 1m (3.3ft) all round as 'turning bins'. Worked reasonably hard they should provide sufficient for the 250sq m (300sq yd) vegetable plot. For a smaller plot build one pair only. Don't make them any smaller than 1cu m (1.3cu yd) to ensure that the rotting goes well.

Other Plant Food

The muck we use is a terrific improver of the soil but it will not always be perfect food for your plants, in particular when they are growing at their fastest. Some years the compost will be very fertile, and in others it may be less well balanced. As each crop is described in this book, reference is made to any supplementary feeds required and these may need to be applied as often as every two weeks when plants are growing or cropping strongly.

We do not use commercial plant foods because they are not organic. Instead we favour either our own liquid manure, or seaweed, or a blood, fish and bone mixture. Given good soil with a good structure, achieved from the use of manure and all the benefits that that should convey in terms of food quality, why not use commercial fertilizers as a supplement? I have to admit that we don't, and again it is a matter of going with your own prejudices and concerns. Our favourite liquid manure is a home-produced one from comfrey leaves, which

TO MAKE LIQUID COMFREY MANURE

Take a plastic water butt or similar, preferably with a tap in the bottom, cut comfrey leaves, push them in, put the lid on and wait about a month. Draw off the liquid that will then have formed, dilute about 3:1, and use.

compares well with any bought fertilizer and is amazingly easy to make. It is high in nitrogen, very high in potash, and has a decent amount of phosphate. The best bought alternative would be seaweed liquid. Growing comfrey is covered in Chapter 6.

With muck, bag fertilizer or good liquid manure there should rarely be deficiencies, but as with growing anything, a good eye for something wrong will help to prevent problems. However, the best results will always be achieved if there is no check to the plants and they are given everything they need.

MANAGING SHORTAGES

The main plant food shortages are indicated by particular symptoms, but can be remedied with the applications described:

Nitrogen shortage: Pale green leaves which should be darker. To redress the balance use poultry manure, blood, dried blood, blood fish and bone, more comfrey liquid, seaweed liquid or seaweed meal.

Phosphate shortage: Poor development of seedlings, or dull leaves in lettuce and sweetcorn. Use poultry manure, bone-meal, or blood, fish and bone.

Potash shortage: Poor cropping, especially of fruiting crops such as tomatoes. Scorching around the edges of leaves especially in gooseberries and tomatoes, chocolate spot on broad beans.

Use better compost (especially in the following year, as in the current year it may be too late), or more comfrey liquid.

Then there are the trace mineral deficiencies:

Magnesium shortage: Pale leaves with dark green veins. It tends to appear most where plants are hungry potash feeders.

Epsom salts lightly sprinkled (or watered) around the plants should redress the balance, at least in the short term; the problem is that it may leach out again quite fast. Dolomite limestone is the long-term organic cure, but I would be tempted to use a non-organic solution if necessary.

Calcium shortage: Flowers falling off, brown patches on tomatoes, curling leaves on potatoes and small tubers, beans failing to develop properly and a purple tinge to brassica leaves.

For calcium shortage use lime. Brassicas in particular like lime, and if there is any sign of purple in the leaves, then lime the brassica plot all over every year. Apply so that the surface of the soil has an even dusting; some authorities use as much as 1kg (2.2lb) to 3sq m (32sq ft), but we find that less is just as effective. On heavy clay soil lime also has the effect of breaking up the surface and should be used when the surface gets too compacted.

It is worth noting that although potatoes need lime, freshly spread it may cause scab, so try to apply it the year before if possible.

Boron shortage: Brown heart in turnips, hollow stem and curd browning in cauliflowers. A little seaweed fertilizer should solve this. Be careful with your liming in future, as this may have been caused by over-liming.

ROTATION OF CROPS

The majority of crops will benefit from a rotation system. Two major benefits are claimed for rotation of crops. One is that pest and parasite build-up can be reduced – though personally I have doubts if many pests are so immobile as to be foiled by a rotation that moves crops a few metres every year; this really applies mostly on a farm scale – and the other is that the soil will maintain better condition and not run out of individual nutrients used heavily by individual plant types. The latter reason is the most compelling, and rotation certainly improves results.

There are two major rotation types: four-crop and three-crop. We had always used a four-crop rotation, but if you use fewer potatoes than we do, then the three-crop may be for you. The three-crop is exactly like the four-crop except that Plots 1 and 2 are merged.

Plot 1: Potatoes, also celery and celeriac; incorporate muck before planting.

Plot 2: Roots; incorporate more muck when the ground is clear after roots.

Plot 3: Legumes.

Plot 4: Brassicas; mulch with muck in October.

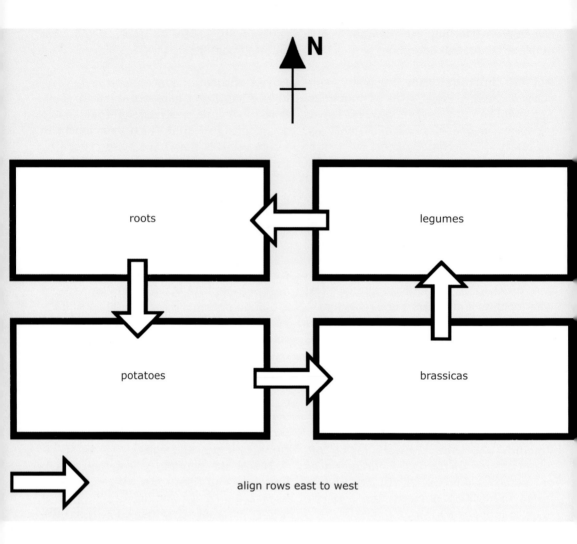

Diagram of a four-plot rotation.

RAISED BEDS

There is a problem with most vegetable gardens, which is that by the time cropping starts you have no option but to put your feet on the soil in order to get to the results of your labours. The outcome of this is compacted soil, which stunts the growth of the remaining crops. In particular in dry parts, by fixing the previously loose top layer to the soil underneath, you lose a mulching effect, and evaporation from the soil becomes much greater.

If you were a commercial grower or growing just for the freezer this would not be a problem as you will be harvesting everything together. If, on the other hand, you wish to pick daily for your own table, the ground soon suffers, as do the remaining plants. Using walking boards can help considerably, but raised beds are, in my view, better still. There is no magic to beds: it is just a matter of dividing the plot into beds that you can reach from paths on both sides. Beds may be, but do not need to be, formally edged and are generally raised simply by the action of digging and incorporating organic material. They need only be a few centimetres high – 10cm (4in) or so.

Most beds are about 120cm (4ft) wide, and are made in soil cleared of all previous crops. This alone can present problems when planning, but as soon as the ground comes clear, you have to find a clear weekend to dig a bed. In a rotation of four or five plots it will normally only be necessary to dig the plots once or twice in a full cycle of four years providing they are kept reasonably clear of weeds. Further muck can be incorporated at various stages by mulching. (Mulching is the lazy way of putting compost or manure on the ground – just lay it on a few centimetres thick.)

For us, beds are made for potatoes, tidied up a bit for the root crops that follow, fed again before the peas and beans are sown – which usually involves digging them over again – then mulched for overwintering brassicas. They are then re-made when the potatoes come round again.

Some authorities refer to intensive raised beds, and because the paths between them bring more light to the plants, it is possible to grow some closer together than in a conventional vegetable garden. However, more plants need better feeding and the preparation of raised beds involves incorporating very serious amounts of good muck into the soil. How much will depend on what you have available, but as a general rule the top spade's depth of the plot should still be more soil than muck (just) and have 3 to 4cm (1 to 1½in) of soil on top for the seedbed, which contains little or no muck (muck may cause very small seedlings to rot).

Intensive beds will also need more subsequent feeding with liquid or other manure. Experiment a bit with these closer spacings; we think that for some crops they do produce more bulk per square metre, but we have generally reverted to standard spacings to get better sized individual plants.

GARDEN FOR THE WINTER, NOT FOR THE SUMMER

As a general rule, growing garden crops sown in the spring for summer and early autumn use is easy. For the beginner, spring is the time to start when results will show quickly enough to give encouragement.

To get crops in the winter (and therefore all year round) requires planning. There is a wide range of crops that can stand through all or part of the winter, but generally they are either in the soil a long time or need to be planted when the soil is full of something else. For example garlic and broad beans are in many areas best planted in late October; garlic is easy, it goes in after the potatoes which will have been lifted by then, but the broad beans have to go on the previous season's root plot which may still be occupied. Planning carefully, if need be using some crops earlier than you might have done or lifting them for storage, can leave a space free. Over-wintering brassicas, so crucial to winter feed, are often sown the previous spring and must then be planted out on the legumes plot (Plot 3, which will be Plot 4 by the time they are to be cropped) while the peas and beans are still there. The secret here is to leave a little extra space between the rows and to interplant.

With just a little protection it should be possible to have salads all the year round. If lettuce and cucumber are all you want in a salad then you may be disappointed, but there is a terrific range of hardier things to use in salad: chicories, some wonderful cresses, claytonia and purslane, to name but a few. These crops, protected from the worst of the frost, will stand and even grow a little on any day there is warmth in the sun; but you do need to grow plenty for a winter's supply.

Protecting Crops in Winter

Protection of your crops in winter can be done through a variety of techniques. That wonderful invention, agricultural fleece in all its variations, has provided the simplest way of just adding a degree of protection; all that is necessary is to lay it on top and stop it blowing away.

The king of winter protection is obviously the greenhouse, and these are expensive if we are talking about enough size to get a decent amount of food from them. However, having invested in one, if it is laid out well to pick up the winter sunshine and with agricultural fleece to aid the fight against the frost, it should be possible to grow good food throughout the year. Problems do occur, however, especially with mildew attack (traditionally known as 'damping off', though I don't know why) largely due to inadequate air flow. This underlines the need for good ventilation or chemical controls, which we prefer not to use. Given that airflow must be maintained now that fuel is so expensive, there really is no sensible justification for heat in a greenhouse.

COMPANION PLANTING

As if planning a rotation were not complicated enough, there is some empirical evidence that planting certain plants in close proximity can enhance or indeed hinder the growth of one (at least) of them. In most cases nobody knows why this may work although theories abound; people just think that it does. Without doubt good husbandry, crop rotations, shelter and above all adequate water have far more effect than many companion plantings, but there are certainly some companions worth considering. If you look at pictures of really good vegetable gardens it is surprising how many of them contain flowers, and I think this is no accident.

You could therefore consider growing the following as companion plants:

■ marigolds (tagetes) to discourage slugs and carrot fly (this definitely works);

■ pot marigolds and any other simple open shallow flowers to encourage hoverflies and lacewings (fennel helps with this too);
■ nasturtiums seem to help tomatoes and brassicas perhaps by discouraging aphids – but they can also smother them, which is less than useful;
■ sunflowers encourage marrows and sweetcorn but are said to discourage beans;
■ petunia and yarrow also appear generally beneficial.

I don't really know whether this works or not, but it certainly improves the appearance of a vegetable garden to have some flowers in it, and somehow it makes it look and feel professional!

Other companions are carrots and onions, the latter thought to help discourage carrot fly; and the beet family seems to do well with brassicas.

**In a greenhouse you can be adventurous, too. Here
a pomegranate is being tried.**

The polytunnel on 29 April, showing peas, potatoes and carrots well advanced.

The polytunnel as a cheap greenhouse alternative is often criticized for being even worse than the greenhouse from the mildew point of view. I don't think they are, however. If a polytunnel is built with at least one mesh side wall to a height of about 50cm (20in), the air flow can be maintained. Obviously this means the building is less able to protect against frost, but using agricultural fleece as well in cold weather will give a few more degrees of protection, which will result in quite adequate winter salad production without mildew.

Because they are relatively cheap it is viable to have a large space covered with a polytunnel, and I like to build cloches or cold frames inside them, too, for extra protection. These must be kept open as much as possible, but on a cold night if the cloches are closed and even a layer of fleece put over the top of those, several degrees of frost can be kept off the plants.

Always grow directly in the soil because this acts as a large heat sink, absorbing heat from the sun as magnified by the polythene (or glass) during the day, and being released at night.

CHOOSING AND PREPARING A SITE

First you should choose your garden for the quality of the view, or the convenience, or whatever gives you greatest pleasure: potentially you will spend a lot of time in it, and the idea is that you enjoy it.

Do not be over-ambitious: it is better to have a small garden well maintained than a large one full of weeds. Beware the enthusiasm of spring. On those first early warm days it is easy to dig enough vegetable garden to be sure of over-committing yourself for the remainder of the year (assuming you do not wreck your back with unaccustomed exercise anyway). Keep it small to start with, and extend it as experience teaches you what time you have available (as well as some shortcuts to do things more quickly).

It is also crucial that you are realistic as to how much time you will be able to spend in your garden, and whether you can make compromises with the rest of your life. If you have only a limited amount of time and wish to cut production to vegetables on 100sq m (120sq yd) or less, then do that – but do it well. Do not grow tough, bug-ridden vegetables in a sea of weeds or the results will never enhance your life either in terms of a significant improvement in your diet or through the satisfaction of gardening well.

Other factors should also be considered when choosing a site for a garden.

■ The growing area must be in full sun for most of the day. Some leafy vegetables can be grown in partial shade, but the need to rotate means that their shade is best provided by other crops.
■ Tree roots impoverish the soil for quite a distance around them. Roots can be pruned but to limited effect.
■ Avoid frost pockets; a slope that has free movement of air downhill is most likely to escape frost damage in late spring and early autumn.
■ A gentle slope facing south or thereabouts helps early crops get started; a steep slope is not good, as most of the moisture and nutrients leave before you have finished with them.
■ Any soil can be productive, especially after improving it with organic matter and anything else it needs. Sandy soils, however, will never be as good as clays and loams, which retain moisture better.

- Good drainage is important, and the vegetable garden should not be situated in a low, wet place.

Preparing the Ground

Breaking in new ground can be done the hard way, the easy way or the wrong way. The wrong way is to use a rotavator, which chops up weed roots and spreads them in the most effective manner possible; in some very dry years a majority of these pieces of root die, but in wetter years some of these weeds really benefit and all the little bits of root grow into nice strong weeds.

The hard way, which I must admit to enjoying, is carefully to turn over the ground with a spade making absolutely sure that, as with an old-fashioned plough, all the weeds and grass on the surface are firmly planted upside down with at least 10cm (4in) of earth on top. This is good exercise for the desk-bound (and quite good for anyone), and has the advantage that quite often the seedbed produced can be used immediately. It really is quite surprising how weed free this system can be, and with a little hoeing you have a plot that might have been there for years. It is also quite good practice to incorporate (bury) some muck at the same time if you can.

The easy way requires advance planning. Lay newspaper on the ground (complete papers, not single sheets) and cover with muck to a depth of 5–10cm (2–4in). Come back six months later and dig or rotavate; the soil will be clean and ready for work.

THE BOUNDARIES

Early in the development of your new plot consider the problems of big pests, in particular dogs, rabbits and other people's children. The damage done by these stray animals can justify the cost of a fence, and since the fence can also be used as a support for soft fruit, apple cordons and other crops, it can be very worthwhile indeed.

Windbreaks

Wind causes the evaporation of moisture from the soil as well as physical damage to the plants, so in exposed areas erect windbreak netting wherever you can to slow it down. After a few months you will be able to look at rows of crops and see noticeable improvements in plants that are benefiting from the shelter. Windbreaks should not be solid, but are designed simply to slow the wind; hence the perforated materials offered. Also these only ever create partial shade, and do not appear to slow growth. Solid boundaries tend to create turbulences which can be damaging to crops as well as creating shade.

As a rule of thumb a windbreak will protect crops on both sides of it to a distance equal to its height. Thus on a 120cm- (4ft-) wide raised bed a windbreak of 60cm (2ft) should suffice if it is placed down the middle, but it would need to be 120cm high if it is down the side (down the side also creates access problems, and the windbreak will need to be set back a path's width and therefore also to be a path's width higher).

Consider big windbreaks as part of a protected growing area. An area surrounded by a windbreak of 2m (6ft 6in) or more high with a roof of bird-proof netting will give a very productive growing area. In summer, 'bird-proof' probably means 2.5cm (1in) mesh net to keep sparrows and similar sized birds out, but in winter such netting may catch sufficient

**The area
protected by
a windbreak.**

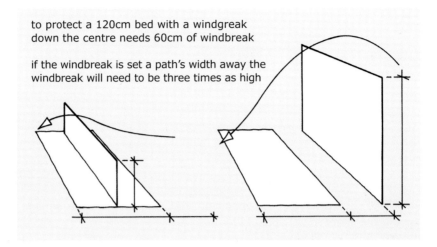

to protect a 120cm bed with a windgreak
down the centre needs 60cm of windbreak

if the windbreak is set a path's width away the
windbreak will need to be three times as high

snow to destroy the whole structure and a larger (10cm/4in) mesh is needed. This still keeps out pigeons, which are the main winter avian pest.

Fences

Despite the obvious beauty of hedges, fences are probably more practical where space is short, and they also present opportunities for crops to be grown on them. The south-facing ones in particular offer the chance to grow all the really glamorous fruit, such as apricots, peaches, figs and pears.

Hedges

Hedges do have their advantages, especially if they can be clipped for feeding to rabbits and goats – though when planting a hedge, please plant something useful; perhaps the worst boundary of all would be Lonicera, yew or some other plant that is poisonous to stock. They may have aesthetic value, but otherwise should go to make room for something more productive. Old hedges, providing they are free of the poisonous items, provide a good volume of clipping from May onwards. Rabbits and goats like hazel, hawthorn, blackthorn, blackberry (despite the prickles) and more.

If you have a problem with tree or hedge roots, the simple solution is to move the plot further away; certainly it is never a good idea to plant within a metre or so of hedges if it can be avoided. Even with that distance it is a good idea to trench the edge nearest the hedge every couple of years and cut back invading roots. You can put a barrier of sheet metal or heavy roofing paper along one wall of the trench to prevent root invasion for several years.

Nut Trees

In gardens with a little more space and which do not need too tidy a boundary, nut trees are a great treat. Their trimmings are also a great favourite with the rabbits and goats, especially in the spring when other green food is in short supply. Clipping too much, however, takes off the flowers, so mainly they must be trimmed only to keep general control rather than being clipped regularly for formality.

MUD

Mud is horrible. Mud is a sign of failure. Mud is a sign of land which is unproductive and is a symptom of bad planning. We are concerned by the aesthetics of the place where we live, so mud will not do when the clients from my other life get invited round to dinner; somehow that gives all the wrong messages!

Our growing medium is good old garden soil. This should never be trodden on and should therefore never turn into mud. This is easy to say and very difficult to avoid, and you will have to lay out your vegetable garden to ensure that you can avoid feet on the growing areas. If you really must tread, then always use a board to spread the weight.

Mud also comes from paths that are trampled and overworked, caused by both the garden farmer and his livestock. In that initial surge of spring enthusiasm, all the paths are put under stress, though luckily mud created at this time of year usually disappears with the first flush of grass growth. Later in the year it just stays as mud. We have all seen squalid smallholdings, usually in the wetter parts of the country, where the mud simply never seems to go. In the most frequented areas it is advisable to put down decent hard paths to cope with the hard use; for those parts where access is lighter and more occasional, and which you would like to leave as grass, make sure that where possible they can be approached from more than one direction. Also rest worn parts as soon as the wear shows. Plan your access points and, for example, have two ways in to your vegetable garden and rotate their use, especially in wet weather.

PEST CONTROL

As a very general rule, if plants do not grow well for you it is a good idea to grow something else, but some pests are ubiquitous, and much as we hate pesticides and other poisons we have to do something. Some level of pest damage is inevitable, but although we are not trying to grow nasty sterile supermarket food, no more are we prepared to accept that the definition of organic is 'full of organisms'.

Slugs and Snails

In our own enterprise we try hard to avoid chemical controls, but we do allow one, the use of slug pellets, because we do not always have the time or energy for beer traps and torch-lit slug hunts. Even so this is a very occasional lapse that we would only use while the frogs and toads are hibernating; this really applies to a few days in the very early spring. Our polytunnel has a small pond in one corner, and within weeks of building it a toad moved in (we also introduced some spawn to make sure of this).

Toads eat small slugs and this is a very satisfactory control, but you cannot use slug pellets as well for fear of damaging the toad, so in this environment we do sink a saucerful of beer into the ground to trap the slugs and snails that Toady does not remove. Under cover, in particular, where the rain does not dilute the traps, beer traps really are very effective, so if you do have the time, use them. Outside, try beer traps under cloches, or similar.

Aphids

For aphid attack we use soapy water which we spray on all plants that look

This frog can come and go as it pleases, controlling the slugs in the strawberry bed.

as if something is living on them. Use plenty, and then you are washing off pests as much as trying to poison them. It is remarkably effective, and exposes us to no more than we expose ourselves to when doing the washing-up. Typically we clear aphid and whitefly attacks with this technique, and often apply it only once in a season. Soft soap is the approved organic soap for this purpose, but I'd rather use dilute washing-up liquid than nothing if we are out of stock of the proper stuff.

Caterpillars

Caterpillars can be a real problem, especially on the brassicas, and when there are more than we can pick off by hand we send away for a biological control that makes the caterpillars very ill and they drop off: very effective, not cheap, but probably fairly safe. Soapy water is not really good enough for these, as once washed off caterpillars tend to climb on again, although with sufficient patience you might pick them up first.

Wireworm

Wireworm is a particular pest in ground that was previously grassland or is adjacent to grassland. They attack most root crops. They are recognized by their wiry appearance, and three pairs of legs at the front (unlike centipedes and millipedes which have 'legs' all along). A patch of spring-sown mustard is said to disperse them. As the garden matures they become less of a problem.

Carrot Fly

The carrot fly attacks parsnips and celery as well as carrots. Techniques for its control are discussed in the carrot section of Chapter 3.

TOOLS AND EQUIPMENT

The general rule with tools is, like buying live-stock, buy the best you can afford and buy those designed exactly for what you want.

The Garden Fork

Without question one of the essential tools. One of your forks, if you have more than one, will end up being left outside in the winter. Daily, we hope, you will be collecting produce for the kitchen, and especially in the winter this will include digging root crops such as leeks, parsnips, late carrots and beet. You are bound to leave the fork out, even if by mistake, and if it has a wooden handle, after a couple of years it will break, undoubtedly when you have no time to mend it.

The obvious solution is a stainless steel one, and there is no doubt that for digging light land this is the nicest tool. However, give it a bit of ground with a couple of tree roots, and before you know it you will be reduced to a three-tine fork. Therefore make stainless your first choice for the second fork, and use it for harvesting and light work. And put it away as often as you can, because even stainless forks usually have a mild steel shaft that is eventually attacked by rust, and it will break.

Number one fork will have to work hard: you will be digging up roots and stones, so look to what professional diggers use. The modern navvy's fork is steel with a composite handle; it is a little heavier than an ordinary garden fork, but it will not rust – and don't worry about the extra weight, because you will find it well balanced enough to use that to your advantage. So go to a builders' merchant and not the garden centre for this one.

Spade

A spade is also essential. Unlike a fork, which you use to stir the soil around to get a good tilth and to release weeds, with a spade you are out to turn the ground right over. Especially for breaking in new or particularly weedy ground in the autumn, the ground needs to be cut into good chunks, lifted and replaced, weed side down. Where ground is to remain vacant over winter, clods may be left intact for the frost to break down into a tilth – if you live in an area where you still get frosts.

Some things are planted in trenches, and a spade is essential for that too.

Your first choice for the front-line spade should be a stainless one. They are not so prone to breaking as forks and they do cut a much better sod, especially in muddy conditions. It may still be a good idea to have a number two spade for rough work (perhaps in particularly stony conditions) made from mild steel, but this is probably not essential for most of us.

The Dibber

Now to that old fork you left out: the broken handle does have a use. Assuming it is 40cm (16in) long or more, put a point on the end of it and this is your dibber – essential for planting potatoes and leeks. Useful, too, as it's probably about the right weight and balance for terminating the lives of rabbits to prepare them for the pot. If you are starting from scratch, use a spare fork handle.

You leave it out, it will break.

Trowel

A trowel will be useful in transplanting small plants to their final growing places. Again, a good stainless steel one is preferable.

Hoes

For all of us growing vegetables, the hoe is a great time-saver. Five minutes with a hoe while seedlings are small saves hours of weeding later. In a wet year, though, there is a problem, because when the ground is wet we keep off the vegetable patch, very properly, to avoid compaction both with our feet and with the hoe itself, which can cause a really nasty mud pie. While we wait for the weather to improve at a convenient weekend the weeds continue to grow, and before you can get back on with the job, the weeds are winning.

Three things can help to reduce this problem. The first, which we have already discussed, is to get the soil condition right: with enough organic matter mud pies are much less likely and the soil returns to normal more quickly. The second is to have more paths and to keep your feet off altogether anyway; and the third is to buy a better hoe. As with spades, hoes are edge tools and need to present constantly a sharp edge either to the soil or to the weed roots. To achieve this in the widest variety of conditions, stainless steel is again the answer.

Hoeing not only clears weeds, it also keeps the surface of the soil free. This reduces evaporation in the summer, and the surface becomes a mulch, retaining water near the roots.

You will actually need two, or even three hoes:

A Dutch (or push) hoe: This should have a blade no more than 13cm (5in) wide (any bigger and you start to chop off the wrong things), and be as light as possible.

A draw (or swan-necked) hoe: This is invaluable when earthing up potatoes as it draws the earth towards you.

An onion hoe: This is a small draw hoe with a short handle designed to be used crouched down around the onion (and other) plants for very careful hoeing work. Whether you use it for that or not is up to you, but when you get into mucking out rabbit hutches there is nothing better.

Small Tools

In addition to the onion hoe, over the years we have collected various small tools to assist in weeding the raised beds. On these beds, where the plants are often close together, these small pronged and bladed hand tools can really help to loosen weeds before pulling them out.

The Garden Line

Take a little trouble over your garden line: if you want to mark out edges, rows or new beds, a good line is invaluable. You probably need two for marking out beds and rows. They are easily enough made, but do use good durable cord without too many knots and snags if you want straight lines. On the subject of straight lines there are many who espouse other systems, but I am still convinced that they are the best possible way of obtaining maximum yields of decent crops for the minimum of labour. Watch the professionals: just because we don't like all their chemical ingredients, don't knock them on all their techniques.

Some of the small tools collection: scruffy, but very useful.

The Wheelbarrow

An increasing number of clever wheel-barrow designs are available and they are all doubtless perfectly satisfactory, but I return for inspiration to those who use these things in their daily work. Get a navvy's barrow: they win on capacity and durability but above all they are well balanced, which minimizes your effort. Again, the builders' merchant is likely to be as good a source as the garden centre.

Watering and Watering Equipment

A few years ago there would have been no question in my mind that a hose was essential to vegetable growing, but several years of hosepipe bans have made us try

to manage without easy water, and we have learnt a lot from the process.

Small amounts of water applied by hose through a sprinkler and wetting only the top centimetre or so of the ground are worse than useless. What happens is that plants develop roots near the source of moisture and if this is the surface, then they become too shallow-rooting and therefore increasingly reliant on being watered. So when you water, get the soil wet.

When sowing seeds use a watering can to wet the drill and then draw dry soil over the top. This mulch of dry earth traps the moisture around the seeds and aids germination. A slight wetting with the hose (or light rain) in the next few days has the effect of restoring the soil structure so the moisture can evaporate more freely, which is worse than useless.

A little frog habitat; one of my favourite parts of the garden.

Cans should be as big as you can reasonably carry. Hoses, if you use them, should be as short as possible to avoid strangling yourself, your family or young crops in their spare coils. There is nothing worse than walking around a good-looking vegetable plot and being assaulted by an out-of-control green python. The solution is to ensure that the tap is as close as possible to the garden; a standpipe in the middle would be about perfect. Remember to turn it off at the mains before frosts, and to drain off exposed pipe runs.

You will need two roses for the watering can: a fine rose is useful for watering seedlings in trays and pots, and a coarser one where larger amounts of water are needed but where plants are still not strong enough to withstand the full flow from the can.

When you do use a hose, ensure that the plants to be watered are watered to a depth of at least several centimetres before moving on to the next patch. Turn the pressure down for young plants; they never do as well when they have been washed out of the ground.

Several irrigation systems are now available that operate on the 'leaky hose' principal, and these seem to be a very efficient way of watering with a minimum of water consumption. Use them for long enough to water the soil thoroughly and then let it dry for a few days before repeating.

The Frost-Free Shed

No gardening book is complete without a reference to this indispensable place wherein can be stored all the bulk produce to keep over the winter. Potatoes, onions, cabbage, carrots, beet and the tree fruits are all major users, but you will also be able to use it for storing dahlia tubers and home-made wine; so make it big enough.

If you are lucky enough to have wonderful stone outbuildings you may have places that require very little attention or investment, except perhaps in a maximum and minimum thermometer to prove the fact that frost never enters. Others of us have to take a little trouble to insulate a shed to achieve this. My own is an old shed lined with boards (walls and ceiling) and with the windows double glazed. I still do not trust it, however, and add an electric fan heater run through a frost 'stat – though in fairness it rarely comes on.

Also stored here are all the spare seeds, which seem to last reasonably well. One tip: test seed that is held in store for viability by growing a small sample on blotting paper like mustard and cress a few weeks before sowing in the ground.

The Propagator

Where seeds need to be started inside for planting out in spring after the weather improves, many seedlings will do perfectly well in a pot, on a saucer and with a clear polythene bag over the pot. That is a simple propagator. For greater reliability, electrically heated ones are available, and they do help especially if you are producing a lot of seedlings.

Remember, these soft environments we are creating for plants give rise to soft plants. They will need to be exposed to progressively cooler temperatures rather than just taken out of the propagator and planted in cold ground. A space in the greenhouse and a night-time covering of fleece will generally achieve this well.

CHAPTER 3

Root Crops

Crop	For us to eat	For rabbits and goats	Pigs	Poultry
Beetroot	Raw, cooked or pickled	A quick nibble but not much use	Raw or cooked*	Best cooked
Carrots	Raw or cooked	Raw	Raw	The odd rotten one otherwise best cooked
Celery and celeriac	Raw or cooked	Raw	Raw	Raw or cooked
Onion family	Raw or cooked	Not much use except garlic in the drinking water	Raw or cooked* plus garlic in water	Raw or cooked plus garlic in water
Parsnips	Cooked	Cooked	Raw or cooked*	Cooked
Potatoes	Cooked	Cooked	Raw but better cooked	Cooked
Salisfy	Cooked; spring shoots in salads	Raw or cooked	Raw	Raw or cooked

* Pig food is subject to legal controls. *See* Chapter 12 before feeding pigs.

This section excludes roots of the brassica family, because all brassicas must be considered together in crop rotations.

BEETROOT

Plot 2. Feed sparingly with comfrey liquid or seaweed-based fertilizer.

If you live in very dry areas and do not have time to water beetroot they will be very disappointing. For years we gave up on them, but recently have had a little more success both because of greater diligence with the watering can and because as the site is worked more the organic matter levels have increased, giving an improvement in water retention. Remember when sowing in dry soil the technique is to water the drills and cover the seeds with dry soil to retain the moisture. Even so, in very dry weather they may be poor.

When you sow them depends on whether you want to eat them in summer (sow in March and April) or store them for the winter (sow in May and June). From the animals' point of view the latter is probably better as they will store in peat or dry soil until required.

When you store them be sure to twist off the tops and not cut them; allow them to dry for a few hours in the sun; and protect them from frost and from mice. Otherwise the instructions on the packet will stand you in good stead.

CARROTS

Plot 2. No additional feeding is normally required.

Carrots benefit from a plot well mucked the previous year; as a result they do well following potatoes. Traditional wisdom has

Carrots with marigolds.

it that if the manure is too fresh the carrots are more likely to fork and otherwise be misshapen. On very light, sandy soils where nutrients leach away very fast, don't let this put you off: we know people who muck this type of soil before carrots to good effect. However, you would not do this on heavier soils, where the carrots really would fork.

There is a wide selection of carrot varieties, but they divide into earlies for summer eating and main crop for autumn eating and storage. If you grow garlic (and you should grow lots of it!) it will come out in time for the last sowing of carrots, and that will enable you to keep the root plot full for the majority of the year. For this last sowing try early carrots again as they mature faster. Bear in mind that carrots are very good animal fodder, so fill as large an area as you can with them.

Carrots have one serious problem: a nasty insect called the 'carrot fly'. Somehow, probably by a sense of smell, these pests home in on your carrot patch and lay their eggs. Out hatch their maggots, which proceed to burrow into all your carrots, in due course making them fit for chicken food only. You may recognize that they have been attacked by a change in the foliage colour towards purple, but by that time there is nothing you can do about it.

Preventative techniques mostly centre around confusing the smells for the adult flies. The first stage is to avoid sowing the seed too thickly, as thinning is bound to release carrot smells into the air. Planting close to the onion family and growing a row of French marigolds around the carrot plot are the most common preventions. The latter is a bit of a bother as the marigolds have to be started in the greenhouse and planted out if they are to be in time to do any good, but we have had some significant success by using them. If you ever want to make a vegetable plot look really special and professional then these marigolds really work, and would be worth growing even if they were totally useless for carrot fly control. String soaked in creosote is another scent barrier that can be used.

Some other approaches use physical barriers such as polythene up to a height of about 30cm (12in). The theory is that these discourage the insects, which are very low flying, but the trouble is that it is hard to avoid it looking a mess. You could also try slightly earthing up the rows. Agricultural fleeces and meshes are also used, and the plants can spend their whole lives under it (if the wind allows); however, I personally have a problem with the look of it.

Other pests include wireworm; *see* Chapter 2 page 31.

Store carrots as for beetroot.

CELERY AND CELERIAC

Plot 1. These plants need well mucked soil.

These two vegetables are grouped together because their cultivation is very similar. Celery is grown for its stalks, and celeriac (also known as turnip-rooted celery) for the root. Celery itself comes either as self-blanching (which is not very hardy), or as the old-fashioned trench-grown type, which is too much like hard work. If you are only going to grow one of these, then select celeriac; we certainly do not use it enough. If earthed up in the autumn it can stand for some months until needed, which alone makes it very useful, and it really is very nice.

The soil for all types needs to be well prepared with plenty of muck incorporated into it. In the spring trouble must be taken to get the plants away well; this preferably involves an electric propagator.

A good crop of garlic.

GARLIC

Plot 2. No additional feeding.

Do not believe those that make garlic growing sound difficult. If you have problems, simply acquire cloves to plant from a different source next time. Buy a bulb of garlic from anywhere you like (we find the best is bought on southern French markets), break off the cloves and plant in the last two weeks of October in rows 30cm (12in) apart, with 20cm (8in) between the plants, about 5cm (2in) deep. Alternatively plant in February or early March, but those planted in the autumn will grow bigger.

Any time after late June, depending on the season (normally mid-July), the leaves begin to yellow. Lift the garlic and lay it (inside if the weather is wet) to dry. When the stems are crisp it can be strung like plaiting a child's hair and looks very decorative.

It is a good idea to grow carrots immediately after garlic as the aroma may keep carrot fly at bay, and in any event that keeps the plot full through the summer. If in doubt, it is worth lifting the garlic a week early to get the carrots sown before the last planting date on the packet.

LEEKS

Plot 1 after early potatoes; they will still be in the ground when this becomes **plot 2.** No extra feeding will be necessary after planting out, assuming the potatoes were mucked well.

The leek is particularly useful as it is an overwintering vegetable that can be used from late summer to spring. Because we do not plant them out until after the early potatoes, and because we have more need of them in the depths of winter, we do not grow them particularly early. Sown generally in March or April, we leave them in a quiet corner until they are ready to plant out. Put the seeds in drills 1cm (½in) deep, cover and wait; they need very little attention until there is space to transplant them. In recent years we have taken to feeding the young plants a couple of times in the seed bed to get better sized plants, but we never feed them further after that. Comfrey liquid is good for root development of all seedlings, and this is our preferred food.

Transplant the seedlings into well dug soil (try to avoid treading on it by using a board if you do not have raised beds). All you need do is push holes into the ground with a dibber about 20cm (8in) apart each way (25cm/10in if you want big ones). The holes need to be two-thirds of the length of the plants to be transplanted. Drop the plants into the holes, fill the holes once with water and walk away: job done. Dig whenever you want them as soon as they are big enough to use.

ONIONS

Plot 2. Prepare a bed with compost and feed a couple of times with comfrey or seaweed for best results.

It is perfectly possible to grow onions from seed, and probably the very best onions are grown this way but they need great care. Two problems in particular afflict onions, and the longer they are in the soil the more likely they are to contract them. The first is onion fly, and this, probably more than anything else, has made sets a preferable way of growing onions because they stay in the ground for a shorter length of time. If growing from seed you can try growing a lot of parsley between every few rows to discourage the fly, but I am happy to buy sets from a source where the fly is not a problem to avoid this one.

The other problem is onion white rot. In recent years the only rain we seem to get arrives just as the onions are maturing, and the base of the plants can go white and they start to rot. If this happens we pull them out of the ground and dry them under cover. Again, the secret is not to leave them in the ground for too long. In a kinder year the harvest is more conventional, and we are able to bend over the tops of the plants as soon as the ends of the leaves begin to yellow and loosen the roots with a fork. Two weeks later they are lifted and put in the sun (or dry shed when rain is about) until dry. We do not string

**Onions. These are an autumn-planted variety
giving an earlier crop.**

them like the garlic (nor do we wear striped shirts and berets), but simply store them in trays in a frost-free shed.

Sets are planted in well firmed soil early in March. Traditionally they were always planted in the surface, but birds seem to have learned how to get them out so they now need to be a bit lower in the ground if necessary for your local birds, as low as just below the surface. Don't press them in too firmly, as any damage to the base will inhibit root development. Space them in rows 30cm (12in) apart, and with about 15cm (6in) between each plant.

SHALLOTS

Plot 2. Prepare a bed with compost.

A modest-looking thing, but the shallot is one of the really noble vegetables. If you don't use a lot of shallots in your cooking and salads already, then try now. They really are wonderful. They are also very easy.

Plant shallots just into the surface of the soil preferably using the best saved from last year as seed. If not, either buy some for seed or simply buy some from a shop as if for eating and plant those. They will grow and multiply during the summer and die back around July. Lift, dry and store. Occasionally shallots go to seed. Cut off the seed heads; the shallots are still perfectly good to use, but they won't keep as long.

Save good, but not excessively large bulbs for planting the following year from plants that have done well. Do not save from plants that have gone to seed.

Shallots.

EVERLASTING ONIONS

Plot 2. No additional feeding.

Forget, if you were ever tempted, the idea of growing Egyptian, tree or Welsh onions. Those marginal contributors to the family are nothing like as good either in yield or flavour as the enormously underestimated everlasting onion. Imagine a spring onion that divides like fast-growing chives, never goes to seed, and even withstands drought: that is the everlasting onion.

If you can get a clump at any time of year, do so. They should be divided up into single plants (not too aggressively) usually about 2–3cm (¾–1in) thick, planted with the root/onion junction about 3cm (1in) deep and 20cm (8in) apart. Water and leave. When needed, dig a clump and stand in a small pot of water on the kitchen windowsill (out of full sun) and use like spring onions both in salads and cooking. Every summer establish a new bed for the following year. We consider it is best to plant them in July and have the new bed ready for use from the beginning of April, by when they have multiplied ten-fold at least, and there is no reason (if you plant enough) why you could not still be digging them a year later.

Spring Onions

We all know and love the traditional spring onion. They are very easy to grow following the instructions on the packet. They do, however, need to be kept well watered to do well, particularly in areas

A bunch of everlasting onions.

where there is a propensity to drought. In some years we don't bother to grow them, relying on the fact that the ever-lasting onions do much the same job for less effort.

PARSNIPS

Plot 2. No special feeding.

For years in our last garden we grew adequate but unimpressive parsnips, and found that the bigger they grew the more likely they were to rot in the soil. Now we are on different soil and grow much better ones. Whatever your soil, we have found it best not to try and sow parsnips outside too early; April is quite soon enough. Parsnips also take a long while to germinate and the seed should be mixed with radish seed before sowing. That way, you get a marker which enables weeding and hoeing to continue, and the radishes will be out of the way soon after the parsnips appear.

An alternative method is to sow parsnips as early as February in deep pots and to transplant them in April. This is a delicate operation to ensure the long tap roots are not disturbed or damaged at transplanting time. The secret is to use loo-roll centres as the pots, then the whole 'pot' can be planted causing minimal disturbance.

In autumn we leave our parsnips in the ground until we need them. Do not eat them until after the first hard frost as they taste soapy before then. If you prefer to lift yours for storage, again, do not do so until after that first frost.

POTATOES

Plot 1. Feed with muck of all types before planting (it must be well rotted).
This is the beginning of the four plot rotation, and it is the time to put a lot of effort into your soil preparation, which will reward not only the potatoes but also the crops that follow them.

Many people say that on the small scale there is no point in growing your own potatoes, and certainly where main crop spuds are concerned it is hard to justify on purely value-per-square-metre terms. That may be true, but I challenge anyone to find a supermarket potato to match newly dug earlies from good, muck-rich soil. Personally I think that applies to the main crop as well, and I simply wouldn't be without them.

For every kilo of good spuds that you harvest there will be at least half a kilo of small or damaged ones, but boiled up these will be great for stock feed. In the depths of winter we use our Rayburn a bit, and that is the best time to boil potatoes for feeding to all the livestock as it costs nothing extra in fuel.

Traditionally seed potatoes are planted at Easter. This tradition really is not helpful since that means planting at any time from late March to late April whether you

Loo-roll centres used as pots for parsnips.

are at 300m (1,000ft) altitude in the North or at sea level in the South. The best rule is to plant about three weeks before the last likely frost; where we are in East Anglia that generally means planting in the second week of April. What we also do is set a few first earlies in the polytunnel and protect them further with fleece. These we set as early as January and hope to crop before the end of April. The advantage of this is that we do not rush and tempt fate by putting in our outside ones too early in the excitement brought by those first few warm sunny days of spring.

Potato varieties fall into three types: first and second earlies, and main crop.

Potato flowers indicating the crop is ready; here in a polytunnel in April.

First earlies: In East Anglia these are generally ready for eating in early to mid June, and a bit later in the North. The crop is light but the flavour so wonderful that the space is easily justified. As they bulk up the flavour of most goes off a bit (they still far outweigh bought ones) and we move on to the second earlies. The ground from the first earlies is generally cleared in July, and allows us to plant the leeks immediately after them, which keeps the plot working well.

Second earlies: Not surprisingly, these follow on from the firsts. In general they are heavier yielding, good flavoured and can stand for a long time giving a supply through the summer. As the summer draws to a close, if there are any left, some of the modern varieties can even be lifted and stored like maincrop varieties. By then, however, I would rather be using maincrop types, as the flavour of those seems to fit the season better.

Main crop: These are the heavy-yielding ones that are lifted in September or October for storing. Here, because they have been in the ground for so much longer exposed to slugs and others, is where the damaged ones start to be a really useful source of animal feed. Separate them as you lift them and store the good ones carefully. The damaged ones can be divided between you and the animals over the next weeks until they are used up. Do not eat any yourselves that are green in whole or in part; get those down the livestock (they'll be in the freezer before it does them any harm).

Varieties of potatoes abound, and you will need to experiment with them to find both those which you like most, and those which do best in your conditions. My parents live on the other side of the country where rainfall is at least twice as high as ours and they have settled on completely different favourites to us. Reading seed catalogues is one of the better winter evening gardening opportunities, and time spent choosing varieties is never wasted.

Unfortunately it really is better to buy seed potatoes every year rather than save your own because disease and pest-free seed is produced at latitudes and altitudes where most of our lowland pests do not survive. It is possible to grow potatoes from 'once grown' seed (that is, to save them from one year to the next) but fresh seed should then be bought for the third year without fail. When the seed arrives lay it gently in trays with the eyes (little buds or bud sockets) upwards in a frost-free place and let the shoots grow. With luck they will be 1–3cm (⅓–1in) long by planting time.

There are many theories about potato planting and I do not seek to discourage anyone from using their own. My technique is to dig the ground just before planting and to incorporate well rotted muck or compost as I go. The muck must be well rotted as potatoes are prone to scabby skins when grown in contact with muck which is still working. The ground should be left with trenches of at least 15cm (6in) deep where the rows are designed to go.

Plant the tubers with a hand fork or trowel to a depth of about 10cm (4in), and try not to step on the soil (use boards or work from paths). Planting distances are 35cm (14in) apart for earlies, 45cm (18in) for second earlies and 60cm (24in) for main crop. The rows should be 45cm (18in) apart for both types of early, and 60cm (24in) for main crop.

The main reason both for the trenches and for having kept the soil structure open and untrodden is that spuds need 'earthing up'. This is heavy enough work without having to wrestle with compacted soil. Soon after they show their heads above the surface, and in every case when there is a frost warning, the soil must be drawn up into ridges to cover the plants. The ideal tool for this is a swan neck (or draw) hoe. This should be done two or three times to ensure that the part of the potato where the young tubers develop is well covered otherwise you will lose half your crop as green potatoes, which are not good for you at all. It should also get you through the frost-risk period and keep the weed seedlings down.

Potato flowers have only one use and that is as a guide to when the first earlies can be dug. Your first crop can be dug when the plants are in full flower. Dig with a fork taking care not to 'fork' them: keep the fork well away from the stems. The first potatoes of the year match asparagus as a delicacy. Cook them immediately, serve with olive oil and parsley (butter if you must) and remind yourself what life is really about! The first few plants may yield so badly that you will have to allow one plant each. Don't worry, this is not a waste, the plants left are busy bulking up and you deserve a treat.

Main crop potatoes are ready when the haulm (top growth) dies down. Commercially it is sprayed with chemicals to make this happen earlier, but if your haulm has not died back by the end of September cut it off anyway. Certainly you want the haulm off before the first frosts. The potatoes then need a few more days in the ground to 'ripen', as this improves their keeping qualities. Try and get them all into store before the frosts take hold as potatoes really do not keep below freezing.

The potato store is worth giving some thought to. It needs to be cool but frost free, dry and dark. So much produce has to be stored in the famous 'frost-free shed' referred to in most vegetable gardening books, and a few ideas are outlined in Chapter 2. The tubers themselves we store either in layers with newspaper in between (so that if one does go bad it will not affect too many of the others) or in paper feed sacks. We check all our stored

Lifting early potatoes.

vegetables regularly anyway looking for stuff that we can 'relegate' to animal food.

One other thought on digging potatoes: do everything you can to get them all out, because the little ones left behind (the chats) carry disease from one season to the next. I have even seen the great Irish potato famine blamed on these recalcitrant little ones and their ability to hold the blight virus in them over the winter and to reinfect the following spring. (The truth is that the virus was much more to do with a lack of genetic diversity, as all Ireland grew the same variety.)

A word on potato blight: this can be identified by unhealthy-looking haulm with dark blotches on it. Usually it appears in warm wet weather. There is no cure for this, but it can be prevented or held at bay by spraying with bordeaux or burgundy mixture, both of which are copper sulphate based. I would say do not use it until you have early signs of the blight, and then spray with it. Without it you may lose the whole crop and the balance of risks from using such a chemical is one worth taking.

Having spent some time on potatoes and extolled their virtues it is only fair to observe their weaknesses, which are that the haulm is inedible and therefore fit only for compost; and that the tubers must, in general, be cooked before feeding to stock. Compare this with the Jerusalem artichoke, where tops and bottoms can be fed raw to stock – but then, most people don't like them much, and certainly wouldn't use them as a staple part of their diet.

SALSIFY (SCORZONERA IS SIMILAR)

Plot 2. A little extra compost will improve results.

Salsify is a great vegetable flavour: some call it the vegetable oyster. Related to the daisy and not to other vegetables, it sits well in the rotation and should be treated in very much the same way as parsnips, although it has a slightly longer growing season. It is hardy and stands through the winter.

Make sure that you have a good depth of soil for best results.

CHAPTER 4

The Legumes

Crop	For us to eat	For rabbits and goats	Pigs	Poultry
Broad beans	Cooked	Not much use	Will eat reluctantly	Not much use
Chick peas	Cooked	Raw any part	Raw any part	Raw any part
French beans	Mostly cooked	Raw any part	Raw any part	Raw any part
Lucerne	Shoots in salad (in desperation)	Cut and feed fresh	Cut and feed	Cut and feed
Peas	Raw or cooked	Raw any part	Raw any part	Raw any part
Runner beans	Cooked	Raw any part	Raw any part	Raw any part
Tares		Cut and feed fresh	Cut and feed	Cut and feed

This section includes several crops normally only grown in gardens as green manures. Here they are grown also, or indeed primarily, as animal feed. All peas and beans 'fix' nitrogen in the soil and therefore leave it in a better state for following crops. Brassicas are particularly hungry for nitrogen, and this is the reason why they follow peas and beans in the rotation.

BROAD BEANS

Plot 3. Feed by digging in compost. They like potash, and wood ashes added to the seed bed will help to provide this.

There is an argument in this house every October as to whether to sow broad beans now, or wait for the spring. If a sowing is made successfully before the winter there is usually a better crop and

These broad beans should be picked quickly now.

the blackfly are less of a problem. The trouble is that the mice may eat the October or November sown seeds! Such is gardening.

Sow in late October (soak the seed briefly in paraffin to discourage mice) and again if necessary in March for what you have lost to the vermin, in double rows 20cm (8in) apart and 7cm (2¾in) between the individual seeds. Seed should be 7cm deep. A second double row needs to be at least 60cm (24in) away both for ease of picking and because you will be planting brassicas in the gaps later on.

Broad beans need some support when they get to about 40cm (16in) high. A few canes and a string around the outside should suffice.

Blackfly really are a nuisance. At the first sign of them (the plants should be nearly fully grown) take the growing points out of anything with blackfly on it and burn. If it happens while the plants are still small, try spraying with soapy water.

Harvest when you like, but in my opinion great big beans taste poor alongside the young ones. Try picking whole small pods, boiling them and chopping them when cool into yoghurt. Serve as an additional salad.

CHICK PEAS

Plot 3. Feed by digging in compost.

Very rarely grown in the UK, chick peas are worth a try. Even if the crop does not ripen properly the plants will make excellent animal food and it looks very pretty while growing. Sow in late April in rows 40cm (16in) apart and thin to 20cm (8in) between each plant. Pick when the pods are ripe. Don't search around for seed, just sow some bought for culinary purposes.

French beans.

FRENCH BEANS

Plot 3. Feed by digging in compost. They like potash, and wood ashes added to the seed bed will help.

Although some varieties climb like runner beans, the majority are relatively short plants. The secret of French beans is to sow them late enough. Garden enthusiasm in the spring is often a problem and it is best to wait until May to sow these. Sow 15cm (6in) apart in rows 60cm (24in) apart and 5cm (2in) deep. Harvest when the beans are about 10cm long.

Never forget to harvest. As soon as the pods get tough and the seeds inside them begin the ripening process, the plants lose interest in producing pods and the crop is reduced. At the height of the cropping season in July and August you will have to pick twice a week.

Keep an eye on the plants, and if they are not holding their beans well off the ground on all sides, provide a short twiggy branch to support them.

There are a great many varieties of 'French' beans. These flat climbing beans are fun to try for a change.

PEAS

Plot 3. Feed by digging in compost.

I have never grown a crop of peas. Don't get me wrong: the plants yield well enough, but a family of grazing animals (four of us) manages to consume most of them before they get to the house. Of those that do make it to the house the majority are used in salads. Cooked peas are almost unheard of, and I must admit I think that cooking them is a waste; they are so good raw.

Peas reward a bit of care. The ground in which they are sown needs plenty of organic matter, as much as anything else simply to supply them with a continuous stream of moisture. Lack of moisture checks growth. If you have the time and energy, a trench a spit deep full of compost or good manure with 10cm (4in) of soil on top would be ideal. Sow the seeds in double rows (as for broad beans) 7–8cm (2¾–3in) apart and 5cm (2in) deep with at least 70cm (27in) between the double rows.

Peas come as early, main crop and others; the 'others' include sugar peas (mangetout) and asparagus peas (another eat-whole type).

In general peas are prone to attack by maggots of the pea moth, which are not easy to prevent. If you get these, then try avoiding 'main crop' peas which tend to crop when the moth is about; instead grow early peas both when the packet says and sow again in late May, and you should then avoid them by having nothing for them to eat at their normal time.

Pea flowers are beautiful.

Pods filling nicely.

If you have a greenhouse, polytunnel or other really sheltered growing space (with cloches), try sowing early peas in October or January; otherwise sow in March, earlies first and the main crop a few weeks later. Sowings can be made for the next two months, and then early types can be sown again in June and July.

Peas need support. Pea sticks (twiggy branches of birch and hazel) are traditional, but we use stout stakes and a length of wire netting equally well. If the support is strong and offers something for them to cling on to, they will be happy. Harvest as soon as the pods are full. Again, delay in picking reduces the crop.

RUNNER BEANS

Plot 3. Feed with compost.

The first job with runner beans is to erect the support. Generally a structure is made from 2.5m (8ft) bamboo canes. Make the structures strongly, as a good row of runners offers a significant sail area to the wind. The frame should enable two rows to be grown about 1m (3ft) apart and for plants to be 15cm (6in) apart in the rows. Not all plants need to grow up canes: strings can be used for intermediate ones.

As for peas, a good trench helps greatly; moisture is important here, too. Sow in May 10cm (4in) deep, and sow a few spares to transplant into any gaps later. Some people like to start their plants earlier in greenhouse or conservatory and plant them out to get earlier crops; I am not convinced that this helps, as too often the early flowers fail and the plants still only get going when they are ready. French beans come earlier than runners anyway, so it is best to eat things in their own season.

Picking is again crucial, at least twice a week in the height of summer. If in doubt about whether a bean is ready, pick it; the problem is if they get too old they get tough, and send a message to the plant that it has succeeded in reproducing itself and need not bother to produce any more beans.

LUCERNE (ALFALFA)

Manure the soil well before sowing. Over the winter a light sprinkling of muck will help.

Lucerne is a wonderful feed crop. Producing armfuls of high value feed from a small area, this crop can be cut at least four times a year. Lucerne is one of the main high protein vegetable ingredients in animal feed. Any excess can be dried as lucerne hay, which again is very valuable feed: just look at the price of it if you can get it.

We sow this in the spring, although it can also be autumn sown, and we do it as early as the weather will allow. In dry years the weather forecast is more critical than the strict sowing date, and we sow lucerne, as many other things, in well watered ground when the weather forecast promises rain as well.

Lucerne can be sown broadcast, but for the sake of weed control, it is better sown in rows a hoe's width (10–12cm) apart. Sow thinly and cover the seeds with just the smallest amount of soil in a deep, fertile, well drained soil. Firm the soil after sowing. As a guide to sowing rates, a gram of seed should cover about 8sq m (9.5sq yd). The crop can be a little slow to establish, but be patient, it is worth it.

Inoculation is used commercially to speed the establishment of the crop. A rhizobium bacterium is used to assist in

Pea sticks. Here the young peas are just showing.

**Traditional bamboo structure for runner
(and other climbing) beans.**

nitrogen fixation. We don't do this, but if you can't get the crop to germinate you may have to.

I have met people whose rabbit production is based entirely on lucerne through the summer, whose flock is reduced to the minimum for the winter when they must feed hard feed, and is allowed to breed again as soon as the crop begins to grow again in the spring. This is not a bad strategy.

TARES (VETCHES)

Tares are a catch crop that requires no additional feeding.

This is a wonderful crop coming just at the worst of the hungry gap in March and April. Tares also feature as a green manure, but as a high quality food the tops at least are just too good to dig in. Sow in the autumn as early as you can after ground comes free from other crops. We sow them after early carrots, garlic and anything else we can get out before the end of September.

J. M. Wilson, writing in 1852 in *The Rural Encyclopaedia or a General Dictionary of Agriculture*, says:

> Most of the annual vetches suitable for field crops are well adapted to cultivation ... for the double purpose of ameliorating the land and affording a supply of fodder. It has even been contended that vetches may be made the means of enabling the arable farmer to support as much live-stock as the grazier. By a judicious combination of vetches with turnips, clover and sainfoin the poor downs may be rendered from ten to thirty times more valuable than they are at present. Vetch ought to be more generally grown ....

He does also warn that if left to stand for seed it may impoverish the soil, but we still may learn from this. There is also some concern, as with so many of the legume family, about the toxicity of the seeds, which are used in some manufactured feeds. There is no problem with the foliage, and that is much more palatable to stock anyway.

Sow on any land that is empty in August and September and which will not be required until spring. Tares do not get away as fast as the weeds, and, especially if you want to turn in a clean green manure crop when you have finished them, it is a good idea to sow in rows a hoe's width apart, 2cm (1in) deep and about 5cm (2in) apart in the rows rather than broadcast and then you can get a hoe through a few times. Weeding them by hand is too laborious.

Pick as required for animal feed. There are, in fact, many varieties of tare but in the UK very few suppliers; look for seed of other varieties when on holiday on the continent. As an aside we find almost always that seed bought on the continent, apart from being much cheaper, germinates with much greater reliability than home-bought seed. I do not claim to know why, but I do think that some of our seedsmen should look to their laurels.

CHAPTER 5

The Brassicas

Crop	For us to eat	For rabbits and goats	Pigs	Poultry
Broccoli	Mainly cooked	Raw	Raw	Raw
Brussels sprouts	Mainly cooked	Raw	Raw	Raw
Cauliflower	Cooked or raw	Raw	Raw	Raw
Cabbage	Cooked or raw	Raw	Cooked or raw	Cooked or raw
Chinese cabbage	Raw	Raw	Raw	Raw
Kohlrabi	Cooked or raw	Raw	Cooked or raw	Cooked or raw
Kale	Cooked or raw	Raw	Cooked or raw	Cooked or raw
Mustard	Seeds	Raw	Raw	Raw
Radish	Raw	Raw	Raw	Raw
Turnip and swede	Cooked or raw	Raw	Cooked or raw	Cooked or raw

All brassicas are on **Plot 4**. The soil should be well prepared from growing legumes on it the previous season. It is further fed by mulching all large plants with compost.

An enormous number of food plants belong to this family. In general they crop heavily in terms of mass per square metre, and are good food for humans and for all stock. They are, however, susceptible to disease (particularly club root) if grown in the same place too long, and the best protection available is your rotation. Production limits will therefore be dictated by how much you can fit into the rotation.

Brassicas produce a lot of food for stock.

Netting is required to keep off pigeons, and it will also reduce the number of butterflies laying eggs on your brassicas and thus the number of caterpillars. Wire netting to the side keeps out rabbits, too, if it is fixed well. Here there is kohlrabi in the foreground, then turnips and cabbages.

Any fertile corner will do for a seedbed providing it has not had brassicas on it recently.

Pests, too, are keen on brassicas; consequently all of these suffer from caterpillars, flea beetle and aphids. Before resorting to the chemical bottle you should consider the variety of controls available which are, I hope, safe. Dealing with flea beetle first: these attack the leaves of plants soon after germination and set the plants back badly. The first control is to ensure that the plants, and the ground around them, are adequately watered, as flea beetles thrive particularly in dry conditions. Next knock them off! If you run your hand along the row of seedlings the flea beetles will jump high into the air; follow your hand with a piece of greased card and large numbers will stick to the card. Repeat as necessary.

Aphids can attack at any time during the summer, and there are many approved ways of controlling them. It is, however, important not to kill ladybird and hoverfly larvae at the same time, as these feed on them; if you do, you will be spraying all summer long. All we ever use is soapy water: wash the plants off with liberal amounts of this maybe a couple of times, and the problem never seems to become too great.

This leaves the caterpillars. If they hatch on a Monday and you don't visit your plot until the following weekend, some of the affected plants can be looking pretty frilly around the edges by then. Having said that, brassicas, in good conditions, recover fairly well once the attack has been stopped. If you are really organized it pays to have a few sachets of a biological control in the cupboard, but if you have to send away for this, the damage will be so much the worse by the time it arrives. Actually it doesn't take all that long to pick off or squash the little blighters by hand, and this is often the best solution; however, if this doesn't appeal, or you really don't have the patience, then spray with soapy water. Use plenty and it will help – but get something else ordered quickly. There are, of course, plenty of commercial sprays that can be used if you choose to; some, such as Derris, are organic.

Generally brassicas need to be sown in a seedbed using very much the same techniques throughout the range, except for the brassica root crops. Plants are then transplanted to the position in which they will crop. Brassicas like good food and drink themselves: they are amongst the hungriest feeders in the garden.

The seedbed needs to be the best part of the plot with fine, moist, fertile soil; in addition, early sowings will need to be indoors. From these early indoor sowings using pots, tray or plant cells and throughout the summer in the seedbed, you should be sowing brassica seeds fairly

regularly. Brassicas are naturally taprooted plants but the taproot gets broken in transplantation and a rootball forms instead. It is important to break that taproot quite early on in the plant's life to encourage a good rootball and achieve good results. This is either done by transplanting as soon as the plant has two good-sized leaves or by just lifting the plants and replanting them in the seedbed at that time if the final site is not ready. Feed occasionally with comfrey liquid (or seaweed) to ensure good plant development.

When you plant out your brassicas every old-fashioned gardener will tell you that they must go into very firm soil. This is, I think, in order to keep the plants tough and to stop them falling over, especially the taller ones. They also caution against feeding the soil with too much manure as the worm activity softens the soil. We feed brassicas as soon as they are established with a compost or manure mulch (which also helps a bit with weed control), and where necessary stake taller plants. Brassicas need to grow fast for best results.

I am not going to pad out this chapter with detailed sowing dates; it is all on the seed packets. Seed for all brassicas needs to be sown about 1cm (½in) deep in drills. If the soil is dry, water the drill and draw dry earth over the top to keep the moisture in.

BROCCOLI

Broccoli falls into two main types: one that grows heads a bit like a green cauliflower, and sprouting broccoli that comes late in the winter. The heading type we find quite hard to grow successfully as it requires moisture and in a dry

Broccoli (illustrated) and sprouts get planted on the pea beds before the peas are finished. They may be held back initially by the lack of space, but in the end they benefit from the nitrogen left by the peas.

year really doesn't perform very well – but when it does it is wonderful. The supermarkets manage to sell this type all year round by importing it from all over the place, but it can look pretty sad by the time you get it home. It needs to be fresh for flavour.

Sprouting broccoli has a knack of coming just when the winter is getting you down. You eat the young flower buds and shoots (some white, some purple) as if it were spring already, and the earlier varieties start in January. Generally this is available as early sprouting or late sprouting. Grow some of the later ones, too, as this can keep you going for a good while, even up to May.

BRUSSELS SPROUTS

'I don't like Brussels', people often say, and I have some sympathy with this. Although, personally, I quite like the old-fashioned strong taste of sprouts, it really can be quite overpowering; however, there is a much greater range of flavours in sprouts than many imagine. Try a few varieties and see which suit you, both for taste and for how well they grow in your conditions. Modern varieties have a much softer, sweeter taste.

Driving around in September and October I am often struck by how much better everyone else's sprout plants look than mine. Very many people grow for an early harvest, whereas we grow for Christmas. This is partly a question of varieties and partly of sowing date – for me, the later the better, as there is tons of other food to eat in October; by December we are into the 'hungry gap' and the sprouts are so much more valuable.

CABBAGE

It is hard to avoid the urge to remind the reader that there really is more to cabbage than memories of school dinners. It is also hard for the supermarket shopper to have any grasp of the range of types and flavours of cabbage available.

As with other crops, the winter evenings have to be spent poring over seed catalogues selecting a range of varieties to be grown. Remembering the general rule at the beginning of the book that we must garden for the winter more than for the summer, it is possible, with enough homework, to produce a steady supply to meet needs throughout the year. Many seed catalogues now give a table of cropping dates from which to select the varieties that come at the right time. We find that in summer cabbages are used very occasionally for formal Sunday meals, but in autumn and winter we cannot get enough. Therefore we select varieties in groups:

Spring cabbage: These are important for filling the May 'hungry gap' when the winter crops have finished and many of the summer ones haven't yet started. They should be planted out in late September from seeds sown in late July. From late April you should have a very welcome early bite, and the plants can then be cleared in time for further crops.

Ones for eating raw: These are usually not needed until the autumn, when salad crops slow down a little.

Ones for cooking: Again the bias, for us at least, is towards winter meals.

Spring cabbage, here ready in mid-May.

CAULIFLOWER

Cauliflower is an excellent vegetable; we particularly like it raw in salads, but it takes up so much space that I cannot grow as much as I would like. Admittedly it does always supply a good crop of outer leaves for rabbit food, but it requires a lot of space; you need to plant each head 45cm (18in) apart in rows 60cm (24in) apart. It is possible to select varieties for an all-year-round supply, but unless you have a passion for it, or garden on the grand scale, select one or two varieties only to mature when you most need them.

If you produce summer varieties remember to protect the curds (the white bits) from the sun; this is normally done by breaking a leaf across the centre of the plant.

The cauliflower is a big plant with lots of green food around it for stock.

CHINESE CABBAGE

Chinese cabbage is more closely related to mustard than to cabbage. We grow it mostly in the polytunnel as it seems to do better with a little shelter (maybe we just water more assiduously in there). Look carefully at the varieties now on offer: there is no need to grow only the supermarket heading types, there are also some interesting open-headed types. Sow in situ and do not transplant. Thin to 30cm (12in) apart in rows 45cm (18in) apart.

KOHLRABI

Kohlrabi just shows how versatile this brassica family is. It is grown for its swollen stem which is wonderful peeled and eaten in salads; cooked it is not worth the bother. The crop can yield very well (as evidenced by the fact that it is largely a fodder crop), but it does need moisture. If grown too dry and therefore too slowly it quickly becomes wooden and uninteresting. It needs to be eaten when still young and tender.

Although we start it in seedbeds and transplant as for other brassicas, this one can be sown in situ.

KALE

Kale, or borecole, is a range of hardy brassicas. Primarily it is a fodder crop, but the young leaves are also very good raw or cooked for human consumption. Transplant the plants to any corner that you can, even if it is 'too late' according to the packet; at the very least there will be a meal for a rabbit on them at some time over the winter. Obviously they must not be put in the wrong parts of the rotation or where other brassicas have been in the last three years, but look hard for corners to fill.

You can either take the whole kale plant and distribute it when needed to livestock and kitchen, or take off large leaves (before they get too old and start to turn yellow, when their nourishing properties are all but gone) and keep the plants going as long as possible. In February and March they produce side shoots, which can be picked off and used like sprouting broccoli.

MUSTARD

Mustard is normally grown just as a green manure, but there is nothing to stop it being cut and fed to livestock, which makes it very useful. The problem is that being a brassica it competes for space with kale and other more important crops. Use only as a fill-in.

There is nothing to stop you growing a few plants for seed and making your own mustard for a bit of fun.

RADISH

We all know how easy radishes are to grow, and that the seeds put in on that first day of the year that feels like spring always do well for an early crop – but as the year progresses radishes are not quite so easy. Like so many in this family they need moisture for quick growth, and fail to achieve this in hot, dry weather. All you can do is to sow some every two weeks throughout the summer and throw away any that do not do well.

Sow radishes like any brassica, but they do not require transplanting and should be ready for eating eighteen to thirty days after sowing. You will be able to sow radish outside the rotation as they are not in the ground long enough to attract club root. If you do this, however, be careful not to leave the runts in the ground.

Winter radishes are worth growing for the root that can be grated into a salad in winter. Again, for best results they need to get away well without water shortage. Sowing time is much better regulated by a long-range weather forecast for some wet weather than by the date on the packet. Sow in position and thin to 10cm (4in) apart in rows 20cm (8in) apart. It is also a good idea to sow these seeds a little deeper, at 2 or 2.5cm (¾ to 1in).

TURNIP AND SWEDE

Turnips need exactly the same conditions as kohlrabi, and once again quick, unchecked growth is all-important. Sow seeds every few weeks to ensure a succession of tender young roots.

Swedes are in the ground a bit longer and normally one sowing only is made. It is a question of luck and watering diligence whether they are tender when finally dug, or whether they are as wooden as a shed door. Grow them as animal fodder with a possible bonus if they are worth eating.

Personally I like neither of these cooked, but if tender they can be wonderful raw. If you like them cooked, great, as you can probably use up some of the less tender ones in cooking. I like to be wasteful and feed any but the best to the livestock.

CHAPTER 6

The Perennial Crops

Crop	For us to eat	For rabbits and goats	Pigs	Poultry
Rhubarb	Cooked	Useless	Useless	Useless
Asparagus	Cooked	Useless	Would be OK cooked	Useless
Globe artichokes	Cooked	Useless	Useless	Useless
Comfrey	Reserve for making liquid manure			
Horseradish	Raw or cooked	Not much use	Not much use	Not much use

I have a list of treats that we would grow purely for self-indulgence even if we were not trying to produce any serious proportion of our own food. Many of them fit in this section; there is a sequence of them through the spring and summer. None of them is worth buying in the shops even if available (with the possible exception of artichokes) because they lose most of their special flavour long before you get them home. In order of their arrival they are:

- Forced rhubarb
- Asparagus
- Globe artichokes
- Sweetcorn on the cob (*see* Plot 5)

Some would add sea kale to this list, and certainly with a bit of messing around it can be forced to arrive very early indeed (depending on the method of forcing used). Personally I think it tastes more like school cabbage than school cabbage and I can't be bothered with it. Do not confuse this with sea-kale beet, which is another thing altogether. I therefore deal with treats first and go on to other perennials.

RHUBARB

Plant in deep, well drained and fertile soil, and feed every winter by putting 4cm (1½in) or so of muck around the plant.

I like rhubarb just as it comes, but for some people it is boring, it reminds them of school dinners, or they worry that the oxalic acid in it is bad for you. If you are of that group, or simply want to try a really special treat, then try 'forcing' it. The flavour will be much improved, and as for the health aspect, it is true that the leaves do contain oxalic acid amongst other things, so do not eat them. The stem is the part we eat anyway.

The usual method of starting rhubarb is to cut pieces of crown from established plants; anything with a bit of root and a leaf bud will grow, and the only attention needed is to ensure that the new plants do not dry out. Do not be too brutal to the donor plant: look for buds growing around the edge and just cut a section out with a knife or a spade. Periodically plants throw up flower heads, and these should be removed as soon as they form. When flower heads become a nuisance the bed is getting tired and a new one should be prepared.

A good strong rhubarb plant but note the white flower head emerging, which indicates the bed may need renewing soon.

Rhubarb is pulled rather than cut, and comes away quite easily. The leaves are then discarded.

No harvest is possible in year one, but in year two you can start. In February before the leaves start invert a dustbin or similar vessel over the crown so as to exclude all light: this is forcing. In the north of England there is a whole industry of forcing rhubarb in sheds, and very good (and early) it is too, but the technique described here is a lot simpler. Now and again lift the bin and look at how things are getting on: after a few weeks and when the stalks are big enough to use, pull them, and put the dustbin back. After the end of May, or sooner if you have had enough, take the dustbin off altogether and let the plants grow on unchecked for the rest of the year. If they end the year looking strong, do the same the following season; if, however, they are looking a bit weak with thin stems, then rest the plant for a year.

Plants that are not forced can be harvested in the same way and will be very good, just not quite so special; we use them a lot for winemaking.

ASPARAGUS

Plant asparagus in deep, well drained and fertile soil. Feed every winter by putting 2 to 3cm (¾ to 1in) of muck around the plants.

Asparagus is the second treat of the season after forced rhubarb. It takes up a considerable space unfortunately, but it just has to be grown. A patch with only a dozen crowns gives a wonderful treat but if you can, grow two or three times that amount. It is usually bought as crowns, which are young plants ready for planting out, but if you have sufficient patience it can be grown from seed. Plants from seed can be a bit variable so follow the instructions on the packet carefully, especially the part about only using the best plants; throw the others away. I have had very good results transplanting and dividing established plants, which is another way of obtaining good strong stock. Asparagus crowns should be treated with care, and in particular they must not be allowed to dry out.

Asparagus can be grown on almost any well drained, fertile soil; the earlier crops come from lighter soils that warm up quickest in spring. The soil should be fed well with muck before planting. There is no point in giving quantities of muck since you will probably be unable to overfeed it; use as much as you can spare. When this is done, make a trench for planting. It will need to be 15–20cm (6–8in) deep, and wide enough to allow you to spread the roots of the crowns that you are planting. The centre of the trench should be raised just a little, and the crowns placed with the buds a little higher than the ends of the roots. Plants should be at least 50cm (20in) apart, and they can be planted in double or treble rows. Rows should be about 1.4m (5ft) apart.

No spears (shoots) should be removed in the first year, and only a few the year after. In year three, tuck in! Remove all shoots for the whole season until 10 June, and then let the plants recover to be fit for the following year. Some experts use a different date in June as late as the 21st or even the 23rd; try it in your own conditions, but for us about the 10th seems to give the plants the best chance and us the best crop in the long term.

Spears ready to cut. An ordinary blade just below the surface will do. Try not to destroy the following shoots by careless brutality.

**Asparagus needs time to recover after the cutting
season. Good strong growth helps next year's crop.**

One cardinal rule with asparagus is to keep the plants free of weeds. If weeds become established, especially perennial ones, the crop will suffer. Add a good layer of muck to the surface every winter, which both feeds the plants and helps with weed control, and you will eat well for many years.

ARTICHOKES (GLOBE)

Plant in deep, well drained and fertile soil, and feed every winter by putting 4cm (1½in) or so of muck around the plant.

Nothing more than a cultivated thistle, these 'superweeds' are an absolute must. Although they have overtones of more southerly climes, some strains grow perfectly well in our climate. There are two ways of producing plants: from seed – follow the instructions on the packet; and from offsets. This has to be the ideal way. Although I have said that they grow perfectly well in our climate, it is true that different varieties are some-what hardier than others, and offsets from successful plants are likely to be from those hardier strains. Also, you get there a year sooner.

As the thistle heads develop through the early summer it is hard to know when, exactly, they are ready. Bear in mind that the plants generally have a main globe and smaller ones on side shoots, which means that the sooner you pick the main ones, the better the side ones will end up. So tuck in, err on the greedy side. Certainly, if they start to show any sign at all of opening into a flower you have left them past their best, so get eating.

Every summer after cropping the plants appear to die and new shoots develop in the autumn. These are slightly susceptible to damage by the winter frosts and should be covered with a light sprinkling of straw,

Globe artichokes.

just sufficient to stop the cold getting to the very heart of the buds. Too much and you are building them into a compost heap and they will duly rot.

Once established, the second or third year of cropping will give you the best yields; after that the plants start to get smaller and less prolific. Offsets should be taken from your established plants to keep your stock young. Take a bud preferably with a piece of root, and separate it from the parent plant. Put it in a well prepared bed (dig some muck in), and wait. You will be surprised how little root you need for success. The books say do this in November (under cover) or in February, but I do it any time in the summer as well to suit my timetable, and it works.

Comfrey can be cut once it is this size.

COMFREY

Plant in deep, well drained and fertile soil, and feed every winter by putting at least 5cm (2in) of muck around and over the plants.

Comfrey must be grown in a corner of every vegetable plot simply for the production of liquid manure (*see* Chapter 2). Select one of the Russian or improved Russian varieties (most of them have the prefix 'Bocking' in their name from the old home of Lawrence Hills who worked so extensively on this plant), and beg or buy small sections of root with a shoot on. Plant them 60cm (24in) apart either way, and leave to establish for one year. Then cut freely for making manure.

So much has been written about the healing properties of comfrey that it would be tempting to grow it for that, too. Read the works of Lawrence D. Hills in particular for enormous amounts on the subject. Be warned also that there are some works by others, which refer to it as a 'serious health risk'. It is not for me to join the debate, as I do only grow it for manure. Having said that, it is spectacularly effective in this capacity.

The plants are grown from offsets. Be under no illusions, if you put a bit of root in the soil it will grow – and if you want to get rid of it you will probably end up feeling not very organic. The roots go deep, and this brings up a lot of elements to make your compost or liquid manure nourishing. It also makes the plants very robust.

In the second and subsequent years after planting all the leaves and stems should be cut off as soon as they reach

Horseradish.

40 or 50cm (16 to 20in) high. In a good year you will be able to do this four or five times. On no account let it set seed or neglect it, as an invasion will follow and in order to get rid of it you may well have to have recourse to the poisons we are trying to avoid.

HORSERADISH

Plant in deep, well drained and fertile soil.

This is an extremely underrated crop. We all know about horseradish sauce with beef – and if you haven't tried it, take it from me that freshly made horseradish is infinitely preferable to the bought stuff – but how about horseradish in salads? It is wonderful. Grate a little fresh horseradish root on a salad and it brings a surprisingly sweet and not too hot flavour, which lifts the salad to another plane.

Horseradish does best on a deep, rich soil that is well fed with muck (doesn't nearly everything?). Avoid shallow soil as it produces rough, forked roots that make food preparation very tedious. To propagate, take a piece of an old plant consisting of a piece of root and a bud, and plant it in a new place at an angle with the top near the surface of the ground. The one problem with horseradish is that despite being easy to leave as a permanent crop (and very effective with pieces of root removed as needed), on that basis you will never get rid of it. Our system is to dig it all up every year, use the large pieces and replant (as above) good crowns taken from smaller parts. Throw away any bits that do not fall into either category.

CHAPTER 7

Other Vegetables

Crop	For us to eat	For rabbits and goats	Pigs	Poultry
Jerusalem artichokes	Raw or in soups	Leaves and tubers raw	Tubers raw or cooked	Cooked
Chicories	Raw or cooked if you produce chicons	Leaves raw	Leaves and roots raw	Leaves raw
Sweetcorn	Cooked	Spent plants raw	Spent plants raw	Don't waste it on them
Cornsalad	Raw	Raw	Raw	Raw
Cress	Raw	Raw	Raw	Raw
Cucumber	Raw or cooked	Not much use	Raw	Not much use
Lettuce	Raw	Not much use	Not much use	Not much use
Marrow family	Courgettes raw in salads other-wise cooked	Not much use	Raw or cooked	They'll pick over them
Spinach and variants	Shoots raw in salads mostly cooked	Some takers	Raw or cooked	Raw or cooked
Tomato	Raw or cooked	Useless	Useless	Useless
Winter purslane	Raw	Raw	Raw	Raw

Most of these crops can safely be planted anywhere in the rotation where you have the space. The only one likely to create any disease problems is the tomato which is related closely enough to the potato to transfer some diseases. These are usually grown indoors however, and that generally gets around that problem.

However disease free plants are, it remains a good practice not to grow them in the same place year after year.

ARTICHOKES (JERUSALEM)

Feed with muck.

One of the most useful domestic feed-stuffs you can grow. The tubers can be dug right the way through the winter (frost permitting) and fed after a quick wash. Unlike potatoes they do not have to be cooked before feeding. Rabbits in particular love them, although pigs seem a little more reserved.

Not only do Jerusalem artichokes produce a good yield of tubers, they don't seem unduly set back by cutting a lump off the tops for animal feed in the late summer. We tend to run a bit short of green feed for a few weeks in September, and this gap is filled well by the tops. Don't cut too much off; we cut them down to a little over a metre high and this also stops the wind blowing them over.

Artichokes do have their weaknesses, and the first is that they are tall and thirsty which means that planting them away from other vegetables can be an advantage. Also when you harvest you will never get them all out, and the following year they will come back like a weed. However, artichokes are very disease resistant and a bed lasting two or three years is likely to prosper. We have tended

Jerusalem artichokes.

to move our bed frequently and in early May we go over last year's bed with a hand fork digging out the tubers as soon as we see a shoot; this does give the stock an extra bite.

The third and most famous weakness is that artichokes make you fart. Sorry, there is nothing I can recommend to solve this one.

Whether the bed is permanent or rotating, all the tubers should be dug up every year and replanted in well manured soil. This can be done any time from November to April according to your convenience. Select the least knobbly tubers and set them about 50cm (20in) apart (in a single row they can be closer) and about 15cm (6in) deep. Could anything be easier?

Yields can be surprisingly heavy, tubers per plant often outweighing potatoes.

CHICORIES

Good soil is needed, but no special feeding is required.

Great in salads, especially in winter; chicories are also a valuable and safe greenfood much liked by rabbits. There are two major types: Witloof chicory, or French endive, which is grown for its buds or 'chicons'; these are forced in the cellars and caves of France. This is quite labour intensive, and although the plant itself is hardy and relatively easy, I do not propose to cover the forcing process here; it is, however, worth growing as animal fodder and just cutting when bulky.

A range of chicories (including curly endive or 'frisee') are grown entirely for their leaves. Many of these can be grown, with some protection, right the way through an English winter, still giving salad leaves when all else fails.

If chicories are too bitter for you, try soaking them in hand-hot water for ten minutes, then rinse in cold; you will be amazed.

Grow according to the instructions; there is such a range of types, try lots.

CORNSALAD

Good soil is needed, but no special feeding is required.

Cornsalad is also known as lamb's lettuce, and is grown much like lettuce. It is another very valuable winter salad plant, but it does have one weakness: when grown under cover it is one of the most susceptible crops to mildew. If mildew is a problem, pull it out and increase the ventilation before trying again in a different place. Also try a different variety. In the end if it remains a problem do not grow it under cover as the amount of ventilation it needs means it might as well be grown outdoors.

Do not be put off however, as it is a very useful winter crop indeed.

CRESS

Good soil is needed, but no special feeding is required.

There are more cresses than watercress and the type grown on blotting paper by children, and all are worth a try. Grow it in rows in the garden like a 'proper' salad crop, and it will produce quite a lot of peppery salad material. The thing that amazes me about most of them is how hardy they are, often standing right through the winter. In particular try common cress (the blotting-paper type) as a salad crop; it grows to over 30cm (12in) high, and is much more flavoursome like that than it is off the windowsill.

When it goes to seed, sow more.

Cornsalad.

CUCUMBER

Feed frequently with comfrey liquid or seaweed fertilizer, and plant out into well manured soil.

There are two major kinds of cucumber: the 'ridge' and the long ones. Ridge cucumbers are grown fairly naturally in that they are quite happy to be pollinated normally, but the other type needs more care as they become extremely bitter and twisted if they are fertilized. Rather than going round pulling off all the male flowers we prefer to grow an all-female variety to keep the work levels down.

The seed for cucumbers has to be started off indoors and planted out either under cover or, for some varieties, in the garden – but in either case they must be protected from frost. Do not grow more than about four plants for a family unless you want to do a lot of pickling, as they all tend to come together. One point to note is that they transplant badly, and it may be a good thing to plant them in fibre pots that they can grow through, rather than in other pots where the roots get disturbed.

Cucumbers need looking at daily to ensure that they are watered enough, not attacked by anything, and that all the fruits are picked off; they are another plant that stops producing when you get behind with the picking.

Keep an eye out for snails and use pellets as necessary, and be sure to pick up and throw away any slugs and snails that you see within a hundred metres of the plants themselves – it doesn't take a snail long to eat through the main stem and kill the plant. And if they are attacked by insects of any type, try the soapy water technique.

LETTUCE

Good soil is needed but no special feeding is required.

Lettuce hardly merits our attention because it is easy to grow and can be grown in any garden. The trouble is that it is the least interesting component of any salad, and the surplus can only be fed to the stock in quite small quanti-

ties. Never feed rabbits large quantities as it is not good for them; I don't understand what it does to them, but occasionally we get livers with white spots on them, and I'm sure lettuce makes this worse.

We grow some lettuce and it is certainly useful; try varieties that stand over winter when you need it most. And be adventurous with your choice of varieties – some of the red ones at least make the salad look nice. Also, try cut-and-come-again techniques, where leaves are cropped from quite small plants: just cut them through 2cm (¾in) above the ground. In due course more leaves will grow, and you can continue the process until the plants go to seed.

Lettuce isn't all boring.

A few lettuces take up very little space.

MARROW, COURGETTES, PUMPKIN AND THEIR ILK

Good soil is needed with plenty of muck worked in. Further feeding with liquid manure is beneficial.

Courgettes: These are just marrows picked before they get big. Varieties should be chosen according to whether, in general, you prefer them big or small – but in any case you will be able to get either or both from the same plants.

Sow them in the ground in May or earlier under cloche cover; the seeds go in pointed end down. We start a few indoors in early April for transplanting every year,

but the advantage is often quite small. Put three seeds in each planting position 60cm (24in) between plants, and when they come up, thin them out to one. Harvest when they are ready. For an earlier crop, sow in mid-March and plant one or two plants in the polytunnel.

Marrows: These really are easy to grow. They can be improved by very good soil and watering if necessary, but even rank amateurs normally succeed with them. For a family we generally plant four plants every year; when things go well we harvest courgettes from them all in the early summer, and when yields get too great leave one or more plants to develop

A young courgette just starting into production.

into full blown marrows. Harvest marrows either for cooking straightaway, or allow them to ripen in the sun off the plant for a week to ensure good storing qualities.

Pumpkins and squashes: You have to allocate a lot of space for pumpkins and squashes as they can be very vigorous plants and spread alarmingly. Trailing varieties of marrow are guilty of this, too. One advantage is that they do grow quite well in partial shade, and we have good results growing them under sweetcorn and other tall plants. Grow as for marrows, but with a bit more space. According to the variety, harvest during the summer for consumption then, or allow to ripen and gather before hard frosts. They keep best in a well ventilated place where the temperature is a little above 10°C.

NEW ZEALAND SPINACH

Good soil is needed; work in the muck first, but no further feeding is required. The soil will be hungry afterwards, so feed before the next crop.

New Zealand spinach is not related to common spinach. It is a large plant, with thick, succulent leaves and stems and grows vigorously, branching and spreading. It thrives in hot weather, and in the dryer areas of England is more suitable than conventional spinach. Sow in rows 90cm (36in) apart and 3cm (1in) deep as soon as the danger of frost is past, and thin to about half that distance. Seeds should be soaked for one to two hours in warm water to aid germination.

Once established, pick off the tips for use and treat as for any other spinach. NZ has one other advantage over the 'real thing': it is lower in oxalic acid and therefore better for you.

SPINACH

Good soil is needed; work in the muck first, but no further feeding is required. The soil will be hungry afterwards, so feed before the next crop.

Some of us might remember the legendary importance of eating spinach to the strength of the cartoon figure 'Popeye'. We are told (in error, as it happens) that this hugely beneficial effect is because of the very high iron content, which must be good for you. However, the truth is that excessive spinach consumption could actually make you ill, as the high levels of oxalic acid in it can lead to calcium shortages. Nevertheless it does taste nice, so why not enjoy it in moderation?

In addition to spinach there are some similar alternatives worth considering, including Swiss chard (see below) and New Zealand spinach (see above), which is more drought tolerant. Both are lower in oxalic acid than the real thing.

SUNFLOWERS

Good soil is needed. Work in the muck first, and then mulch with good muck when established if you have it spare.

Ordinary sunflowers, such as the children grow for the tallest sunflower competitions, will do perfectly well, or use some seed saved from the bird food. Sow them in good soil as soon as the frosts have passed, and leave them until the heads are browning and hanging down. If you are unlucky, the greenfinches will move in the week before and eat the lot, but otherwise cut them and hang them out of the way of vermin to feed to rabbits and hens as a good healthy oil and protein supplement to their winter diets.

SWEETCORN

Good soil is needed with a lot of muck worked into it. Also feed with high nitrogen fertilizer.

Sweetcorn is on my 'treats' list, and is not the easiest crop to grow well in England. It is necessary to buy hybrid varieties (others are available but do not normally produce the flavour of the hybrids) and to start them in early April under cover. Plant out in early May. Corn is a hungry eater and tells you when it needs more: keep an eye on the colour of the leaves, and if they are anything other than dark green, then you have underfed it. The food required is nitrogen, so select from blood, dried blood, seaweed meal or comfrey liquid. Results should show within days.

Corn is wind pollinated and should always be grown in blocks rather than rows in order to maximize pollination. The corn cobs form in the joint between a leaf and the stem. They are themselves covered in a fairly thick layer of leaf-like material, and it is therefore not easy to tell when they are ripe. A tassel eventually comes out of the end of the cob and this dries to brown when the corn cob is ready; gently peel back the covering and check that the seeds on the cob are all golden yellow in colour. If they are still pale, cover and wait for another week.

Sweetcorn cob just filling out showing the 'tassels'. Tassels turn brown just a few days ahead of the cob's ripening.

SWISS CHARD

Good soil is needed; work in the muck first, but no further feeding is required. The soil will be hungry afterwards, so feed before the next crop.

Although not on my all-time favourite treats list, this one is still worth growing – in fact it is very close to a place on the list. Swiss chard is a type of beet that has been developed for its tops instead of its roots. The leaves are harvested and used as spinach. Sometimes we separate the central rib, which is firm, wide and white, cooking that as 'poor man's asparagus'. There is also a red variety, with a red rib; you could try it, though it does not do so well for us. The plant crops well but does eventually go to seed, so we sow twice a year to ensure a progression.

When chard does go to seed, cut out all the ribby bits and the stems that are still tender before chucking the rest to the pigs or on the compost heap. I think this is slightly less 'poor man's' asparagus than the leaf ribs. Boil until tender and try

Swiss chard.

dressed in olive oil with a dash of lemon.

Grow in the same way as beetroot (to which it is closely related), but thin out to 15cm (6in) apart. Make two sowings, one in the spring and another in July or August, which should see you through the winter.

PERPETUAL SPINACH OR LEAF BEET

Good soil is needed; work in the muck first, but no further feeding is required.

The soil will be hungry afterwards, so feed before the next crop.

This is quite a useful spinach and stands for a good long season including over winter. It is easy to grow; the instructions on the pack are all you need.

If you have the patience it is well worth putting a cloche over some early in the spring or growing it in the greenhouse, as the fresh shoots can be used in salads.

There are hundreds of varieties of tomato, and flavour varies a great deal. Experiment a little. We find that the ugly ones (here 'Cour de Boeuf') are often the most flavoursome.

TOMATOES

The soil must be prepared with a lot of muck; when the fruit is set, use comfrey liquid or seaweed fertilizer as often as two or three times a week.

Most tomatoes are grown under cover, but many varieties will do reasonably well outside. There is no doubt in my mind that the outdoor grown ones have an infinitely superior flavour. We do grow some under cover because they are earlier, but the outside ones when they arrive are always the favourites.

Started indoors following the instruction on the packet, plants will always be ready to go outside just before you feel safe about frosts. Even so, when they are ready they must go out; just protect them all you can with fleece (several layers if need be) and hope. We tend to sow seeds in at least two batches so that if the first are slaughtered by a late frost we can revert to the others. When growing on a windowsill, try to get the maximum of light to the plants otherwise they will become drawn and perform poorly. Tinfoil supported behind them to reflect sunlight can help a great deal.

When planting them out, also plant a good strong stake or other means of support (we use strings from the roof of the polytunnel buried beneath the plant) at that time to avoid root disturbance later. Plants will need to be tied gently to the stake every week or so when growing fast; allow plenty of growing room or the stems will be seriously constricted by the strings.

The other great tomato job is pinching out side shoots. There are some varieties that claim to grow well as bushes, but for most it is important to train the plant as a single stem with trusses of flowers on it; bushes tend to lay their fruits on the ground for the slugs to eat. Side shoots generally appear at the base of the leaves, and they should be removed as early as possible before too much of the plant's energy has gone into them.

The biggest disease problem is blight. If you see brown marks on the leaves like cigarette burns, you have it. Clear the plants immediately, burn them or take them to the tip and try again next year. Do not delay (or leave dropped tomatoes about), especially if next year potatoes are following on the same land.

WINTER PURSLANE

Good soil is needed, but no special feeding is required.

Another useful winter cropper, especially with a little protection; it grows now as a weed in our polytunnel, but being fairly shallow rooting, is easy to control. It produces bunches of round leaves on stalks, and although the flavour is not exciting, it helps to bulk up a winter salad and acts well as a foil to the chicories if they become a bit strong. It is perfectly good as animal food when cleared out in the spring.

CHAPTER 8

Fruit

ORCHARD CROPS

For all tree crops, muck as well as blood fish and bone meal should be worked into the bottom of the planting hole. Give an occasional mulch with muck.

We are not seriously talking about orchards in this book, since the size of plot we are dealing with is generally too small to allow for large trees. Nevertheless in the last fifty years so much work has been done on fruit tree development that even commercial growers have grubbed out their old large fruit trees and replaced them with smaller ones; and there are smaller varieties still. Using the edges of the plot for growing cordons, walls and fences for espaliers or just very small rootstocks, even quite small plots can grow apples and, to a lesser extent, plums and pears (which still tend to be a bit big).

The trouble with fruit trees is that a certain amount of care is essential in two main areas. The first is that every winter you will have to spray them with something; and the second is that they have to be pruned, which requires some skill.

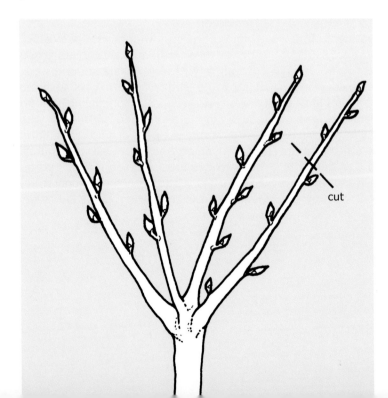

cut

Prune to an outward-facing bud.

Although prunings and windfalls are all good animal food, the animals must not be allowed free access to the trees. This tree will not recover from its sheep damage.

Traditionally trees are sprayed with a tar oil wash, with no danger of it being toxic to humans since it is applied in the dormant period months before any fruit is harvested. Follow the instructions on the tin, making sure that everything is properly wetted with the mixture. In years where you do not do it you will have more trouble from aphids, mildew, scale insects and a myriad others: it is one winter job that just must be done.

Pruning, too, is mainly a winter job, and our objective is to keep it as simple and quick as possible. There are plenty of excellent specialist publications to guide you through training fruit trees as cordons or espaliers and other detailed operations. We need to consider only that trees need to be pruned so that there are no crossed branches, and all the branches that are left can see the sun. You need to prune between one third and a half of the previous summer's growth off each shoot for an established tree.

Pruning in winter tends to stimulate growth; pruning in late summer after fruiting tends to stimulate fruit. Hence when a tree is young, winter pruning is important, and for older trees summer pruning may be more useful.

Summer prunings of most fruit trees can be fed to rabbits and more particularly to goats. Windfalls and damaged fruit go to the pigs (actually apples and pears go to the rabbits and goats as well if they are not too bad).

Apple

The king of the fruit trees has to be the apple. There are hundreds of different varieties, and there is nothing better than a good apple for proving how short-changed we are for choice in the super-market. Choose varieties primarily for taste; go to the national collection at Brogdale once or twice in the late summer and try them. Apart from being a fasci-nating day out, there is no other way of getting the choice.

Commercial growers choose varieties for their resistance to damage in handling and transport and their ability to store them. We don't have to – indeed, who cares how well they store (except perhaps the latest varieties)? On our scale you won't be storing many at all, as we prob-ably cannot aim for self-sufficiency in fruit: whereas in vegetables you may get quite close to providing all your needs, if you eat enough fruit to be healthy it will be difficult to produce enough, especially for the winter. There can, however, be quite a long season for apples, and a succession of varieties through the season should give apples from late July and into November before you need worry about storage.

One factor which must always influence your choice of fruit trees is pollination. Various apple trees have to be grown together in order to ensure that the polli-nating insects transfer pollen from the flowers of one tree to the flowers of another. Since not all trees flower at the same time, the selection has to be made

Apples, the king of tree fruits.

to ensure that two always do. This is not as daunting as it may first seem to be, as nurseries generally group trees into categories in their catalogues for easy reference.

The other choice you have to make is the rootstock, since the type of rootstock dictates the size and vigour of the tree. Clearly the bigger the tree, the more apples you can get, but big trees are unlikely to be possible on the garden scale. In any case there will be large numbers of apples that you cannot reach and which are therefore wasted; also large trees take a long time to start yielding. Thus the largest rootstock you should normally consider is the commercial one known as MM.106. The larger ones are called MM.111 and M.2, and we need not consider them further.

To refine the decision we then have to decide whether to grow trees that look like trees (and if so, how big they are to be), or cordons (a living fence of trees) or espaliers (fan-trained to a wall). Within these categories are many variations and refinements, but at this stage the general categories will do.

In addition to MM.106 there are three other alternatives: M.26 (smaller), M.9 (smaller still) and M.27 (tiny). The problem with the smaller ones is that they tend to be fragile except for a few very vigorous varieties. They must always be staked, fed well, kept weed free around the base, and you cannot grow crops too close to them as they will lose out in competition with them. As a general rule if you can fit in M26 or M.106 this is probably the best. Assuming that within the garden most fruit will be grown as cordons or espaliers, where the plants are to be trained it is important to stick with the stronger rootstocks, unless space really is an issue.

Pears

Pears are simpler because there is less choice. Two rootstocks only are generally available, known as quince A and quince C. The size of the tree, if grown as a tree, is in both cases around 4m (13ft) in diameter, although C tends to be smaller (and less productive) than A. Once again, trained plants make better use of limited space.

Pollination is an issue, as it is for apples; although some are sold as self-fertile, they still usually do better with a pollinator.

Refer to specialist books for pruning.

Plums

Like pears, there are only two rootstocks to choose from: St Julian A and Pixy, with space requirements of 4m (13ft) and 2.5m (8ft) respectively. Plums are less commonly trained than apples and pears, but it can be done. On our scale the fan-trained plant grown against a south- or west-facing wall is particularly successful.

Nuts

Perhaps nuts should not be taken too seriously as a garden crop. Certainly to get the best of them you need to space the trees well, as if for an orchard. Yields will never be spectacular in terms of bulk, and, if squirrels are in your area, you will have a job to keep any at all.

Where nut may have a value is if you have a boundary of a type that could be described as 'informal'. As a rough hedge, nut trees do well (they also lay well into a good hedge, but that is another subject and laying spoils the crop) and whilst the yields of nut from a hedge are never great, it is more productive than ever the dreaded Leylandii could be.

A Victoria plum in June showing, as with most fruit trees, that it is selecting the fruit to develop and to drop. Three weeks later there will only be one on this branch.

Figs

If you have a south- or west-facing wall not already growing crops, then plant a fig. They are purely for indulgence, but if you like fresh figs as much as I do you will grow one.

The main chore with figs is simply keeping them under control. This has to be done not only to ensure that the fruits get the best of the sun, but in order to get any fruit at all it is necessary to restrict the plant's roots. If you do not, you will get a very vigorous (not to say invasive) plant, but no crop. The main technique for controlling figs is to plant them so that their roots are restricted by lining the planting hole with a large old drum or paving slabs. A half-metre cube is about the right size, and don't forget good drainage holes in the bottom of any vessel. Further restriction comes from pruning.

Figs produce two crops of fruit every year. The first is produced in the spring, and because our summers are really too cold for figs, they fail. In fact it is a good practice to pick them off in the late autumn and throw them to the pigs. Late in the summer the second crop develops, and with reasonable care on a sheltered site these make it through the winter to ripen the following summer.

Figs. These are actually summer figs, but because they are grown inside they will ripen in most years and are not likely to be pig food.

After planting, the shoots should be pruned to less than half their length, to just above a good bud. The following summer leave it alone, and the spring after that remove branches growing in the wrong place and shorten back the remainder once more. Thereafter it is only a matter of pruning each spring to keep the plant under control; there is no sense in allowing branches that do not see the light as they will never crop well.

SOFT FRUIT

Generally speaking all soft fruit is grown outside the rotation plan and therefore the quantities are often decided by the available space. Soft fruit, more than anything else, falls prey to birds, wasps, children and other pests, and a fruit cage can be a good investment.

Soft fruit is going to be in one place for a long time, so stop and think whether that space will really be free for ten years. Ensure that the site is truly free of weeds. Anything that comes through of a deep-rooted nature is going to be virtually impossible to get rid of once the plants are in. Particular problems will be bindweed, ground elder, nettles and couch. Rather than spray with weedkillers, try the newspaper technique in Chapter 2 and wait a year or two before planting. It does require advance planning, but is also very effective.

In general there are no great benefits to the livestock from growing soft fruit except that some prunings are good fodder when they occur; nothing is poisonous, so give it a try. They are grown mainly for your pleasure.

Strawberries

The soil should be well prepared, incorporating muck. Liquid feed after cropping will help develop strong plants.

This is perhaps the most disappointing fruit in the world; we all know what to expect and are usually disappointed by shop-bought fruit which delivers hard, 'cold'-tasting fruit with inadequate perfume. There is usually just enough of the smell to remind you what a good one would taste like if only you could get hold of it.

This is in our hands. Forget the commercial varieties such as 'Cambridge Favourite' and many of the other names out of the catalogues, and go flavour hunting. Do not expect the local 'pick your own' to yield useful information about varieties, and remember that flavour also varies according to growing conditions. Start by asking friends and neighbours if you can try theirs, but be warned: people do not like it when you decline runners (young plants) from their stock just because, in your view, they are still not as special as the ones you are searching for. If you are unsuccessful in this, then the catalogues will have to be used to find a variety that appeals – though not surprisingly, the vendors usually speak highly of most of their varieties. Try 'Royal Sovereign': many claim it to be the best flavour, or 'Marshmellow', our own favourite.

There are two main types of strawberry:

- Types propagated by runners. Runners are baby plants that grow on a long shoot that appears in strawberry beds throughout the summer. For propagation these should be removed and planted into next year's site in late summer.
- Alpine or forest types. These always have a better flavour, but the berries are small and yields are not high. Some of the improved ones are beginning to yield a little better and may be worth

A nice strawberry. I can't remember the variety; these were propagated by runners from a friend.

A WORD ABOUT VIRUS

A brief word about virus. There is a certification scheme which guarantees that stock you buy will be virus free, the implication being that if you are given runners by a neighbour they will not necessarily be free of these viruses. I suggest that you need take no more than reasonable care in order not to bring on to your land diseased plants of any type, and that strawberries are no exception. As long as you observe that basic care, and also a reasonable rotation of the strawberry bed (a new site every three years is a good plan), you should be all right. I'm sorry to be cynical, but these schemes seem to me to offer a remarkably good marketing opportunity to the growers.

looking at. No runners are produced, so these are usually grown from seed.

They do have the advantage that they look good grown around the edge of borders in the decorative garden.

Amongst the mainstream varieties there is also a range of cropping period, and it may be an advantage to grow at least two varieties for the longest possible production span.

Having obtained your runners they need to be planted in humus-rich, well drained soil 40cm (16in) apart in rows 80cm (32in) apart. Keep the plot free of weeds, and when fruiting starts, lay a little straw around the plants to keep the fruit off the ground when it gets heavier. This will create a great environment for slugs so unless your frogs and toads are active you may have to sprinkle a few slug pellets underneath.

In the last few years we have been given some yellow alpine-type strawberries. Everyone should grow some of these as the birds do not eat them. They may get wise one day, but until they learn, yellow strawberries are a much easier crop albeit a small one.

Raspberries

Muck as well as blood fish and bonemeal should be worked into the planting hole. An occasional mulch with muck is also necessary.

There are two distinctly different kinds of raspberry: summer fruiting and autumn fruiting. Just as for strawberries, I like to acquire my fruit bushes from friends and others whose crops I admire – and again, the disease issue is used by growers to encourage you to buy from them. You decide: I think we can all identify really healthy plants, but if you prefer to be cautious, try the growers.

Plant new plants (canes) in well prepared trenches at the same level as there were plants before. Do this when the plants are dormant – November is ideal. Do not be surprised that roots are often quite small on the suckers that you are planting. When planted, cut back the canes to 10cm (4in) above the ground.

Raspberries need fences to support them, ideally horizontal wires at 40cm (16in) intervals above the ground, to which they can be tied. There are many variations on this theme, but any good support will work.

Pruning is different for the two types. In autumn, the summer-cropping types have all their old wood cut out and the best of the new growth tied into the fence. For autumn-fruiting types, all canes are cut down in late winter and the best of new growth tied in during the summer (the weaker growth is removed).

Blackcurrants, Redcurrants and Whitecurrants

Put muck as well as blood fish and bonemeal in the planting hole. Plants will need an occasional mulch with muck.

Blackcurrants are planted 1.5m (5ft) apart and cut back after planting to an outward-facing bud about four up from the ground; this leaves a very bare-looking plot. No cropping will happen until year two. In the meantime, use the space in between for salad crops and summer vegetables. Red- and whitecurrants can be planted closer together – about 1.2m (4ft) – and are cut back somewhat harder than their black brethren.

Pruning is a winter job. For blackcurrants, the best fruit is grown on last year's wood, so never cut that back. Cut out all three-year-old growth to a 2cm (¾in) stump and trim any two-year-old growth

Raspberries cropping well.

Redcurrants; probably the best crop we've ever grown.

Tayberries.

necessary to keep the plant reasonably open.

For red- and whitecurrants the treatment is different. These should have leaders trimmed back, leaving about 8cm (3in) of last year's growth. Laterals should be reduced to one bud. Old, unproductive wood needs to be cut out for these, too.

Aphids can be a problem. As with all fruit trees and bushes, the same tar oil wash used for the apple trees in the winter should be applied to minimize the risk, but if the attack comes, spray immediately with soapy water.

Blackberries, Loganberries and Other Climbing Hybrid Berries

These berries do not take advantage from any supplementary food, but organic

Gooseberries. Note a few distorted leaves from an earlier aphid attack. Soapy water cleared the worst of it, and the plants recovered well enough to crop.

matter in the soil will help if only to retain moisture.

These have to be grown around the edge of the plot otherwise they take up too much room. They need to be trained along a fence, and with care can make a useful windbreak as well as giving a wonderful crop. Most varieties need to be planted 2.5m (5ft) apart, although some of the very vigorous ones need more; they also need to be trained along wires at least 30cm (12in) apart vertically. Use insulated wire if you can, as it is a little softer. Every winter tie in the best of the new growth,

cutting out the weaker of the old growth as necessary to make way for it; shoots can fruit for several years.

The object of the exercise with plants such as these, which can be very vigorous, is to avoid the creation of a bramble patch. Not only do bramble patches take up too much space, they only crop on the outside.

Gooseberries

Put muck as well as blood fish and bone-meal in the planting hole. Also, give an annual mulch with muck.

Gooseberries are generally best grown as bushes; follow the same procedure as for blackcurrants, with a 1.2m (4ft) planting distance. They are somewhat hungrier feeders than the currants, and an annual mulch will help them to grow well.

Pruning is mostly about self-preservation. A wine-glass shape of plant will reduce the number of scratches suffered in picking and get the sun in to ripen the fruit as well.

Sawfly larvae attack ours frequently, and in a very short space of time they can eat large numbers of leaves; left too long they can eat them all. Spraying with soapy water seems to get them off the plants, but never put it off until the next day because of the speed of the attack. As soon as spraying is finished, hoe around the plants to stop them climbing back on, because all too often they do just that.

CHAPTER 9

Introduction to Livestock

The livestock section deals with several diffi-cult issues. The first is that, in addition to eggs and milk, we are talking about meat, and meat means killing. I strongly advise that even before you start, you plan and prepare for how the killing will be done. There is an option with hens and maybe ducks just kept for eggs, that you either keep them as pets until they grow old, or re-home them when their work is done. If this is your plan, great, but otherwise killing has to be planned for.

There are two main options: either all your animals are processed for you by a butcher, or you kill them at home. Even the first is not as easy as you might think, as most butchers do not kill for themselves but collect meat from the abattoir where the animal has been killed, and then just cut it for their shop. However, many will help you with poultry and rabbits, so it is as well to make contact with one very early on in your planning.

Killing at home is perfectly possible, but there are several legal hurdles to over-come. You will need equipment and you will need guidance. This can come from a licensed slaughterer, and there are still some who will travel around and help with this. You will have to ask around among other smallholders to find these people, but they are really useful to know.

THE COMPONENTS OF FEED

Protein

Our second issue is protein. Modern farm animals are expected to work hard: they must grow fast, and lay ever more eggs or produce ever more milk in order to maxi-mize profit (indeed, too often for the farmer's very survival). Stock feed is therefore manufactured to provide all the necessary inputs to balance the required outputs. And however efficient the animals become from selective breeding, cloning or other genetic fiddling, they cannot produce as much from low grade food as they can from high grade food. The main effect of this is that the foods used have very high protein levels, and these are obtained by adding protein supplements to the basic ration (usually cereal or grass).

Protein is therefore crucial and valuable, and is why old cows have been rendered down and fed as a component of stock feedstuffs to their daughters, and prob-ably why spongiform encephalopathies (BSE) and scrapie have come to haunt us. The practice above has now been outlawed, but 'old animal' is still on the menu for other stock – and this is surely right, otherwise we waste valuable natural resources. Feedbags are now labelled so that this can be avoided by those who wish to do so. Bag labelling requirements in general are now quite useful, and certainly help in our search for foods that match our preferences.

Whatever we decide is acceptable to us in terms of a protein source, protein we must have. The greatest failure of all is to fail to feed stock adequately, and protein sources must be found. Even if stock animals are being fed and/or bred to grow a little more slowly, they must not be undernourished. You will need to make some compromises, but at least you are in some control of the decision.

The proteins available in 'bag feed' from the feed merchant mostly carry some risks; these are indicated in the table below.

Protein sources	Risks
Soya	Now commonly genetically modified. Huge areas of rainforest have been sacrificed for this crop, underlining the price we pay for protein.
Lucerne	I have not heard of any risks connected to lucerne, and would consider it as safe. It is not grown enough in the UK. For those growing it on a larger scale, lucerne as a crop to feed directly to stock in summer and as hay in winter, would answer almost all concerns.
Milk and milk wastes	All the evidence is that this is safe protein, but it is, of course, expensive protein having come from a cow that was itself fed protein. Use it if you have it.
Mechanically reclaimed meat and other animal products	People don't seem to like the idea of this process. Personally I find this less worrying than many other protein sources, and it seems to me to be good waste recycling.
Fish and fish waste	Farmed fish is fed a colorant to keep the meat that may appear in fish waste pink in colour. There is huge concern about environmental depletion from the factory ships. Also the flavour of some meat and eggs can be tainted by being fed fish.

Feed Additives

Our third issue is feed additives. Additives that are used include growth enhancers such as copper and antibiotics, egg and fish colour enhancers (this stuff may even occur in rations for free range poultry, and there have been fears on the effect of this forming crystals in children's eyes) and, as with too much other food, food preservatives. Much of this may be perfectly safe, but we start from a position of concern.

Both organic food and additive-free feeds are quite widely available, although finding them does take a bit of effort sometimes, and they are more expensive. Sadly, even with our best intentions, these feeds also push up the market value of protein and make it ever more worthwhile to fell rainforest so as to grow more soya.

Most of the feed that is easily available is manufactured either for modern farming methods or for pets. Pet foods are usually unsuitable because they are aimed at animals that do not work as hard as animals used for serious production – in other words, the protein content will be too low.

Commercial feeds are very scientific, and whatever we may dislike or distrust about the industry, it must be recognized as being sophisticated, modern and skilled. For our purposes, one commercial product is worth looking out for: many commercial producers, having put additives into the ration for the majority of an animal's life, also produce an additive-free alternative that can be fed in the weeks before slaughter. I hope that these are always used commercially when they should be! These feeds suit our requirement well, and on our small scale may be used throughout the animal's life.

Just a word of caution: if you live close to a major commercial livestock production unit and decide to keep the same species in your garden, if you do not use antibiotics you run a high disease risk to your own stock.

In the end, every bag of food that you buy has some environmental or health risk attached to it, and you must either accept those risks, or dilute them, or find something else altogether to feed to your stock. What you may have available is food waste. Once again, the law raises

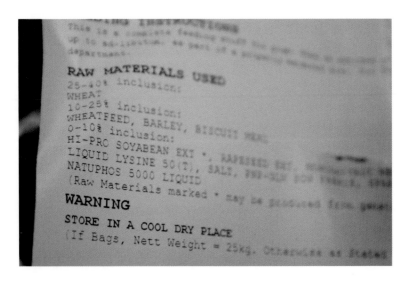

Feed bags are all labelled. It's just a case of understanding them!

some difficulties, but all waste that can be recycled helps. We humans generally have a higher protein diet than we should, considering the work we do, so our waste food is often quite useful for our stock.

Perhaps the ideal way to reduce all risks and concerns is only to keep a few hens or ducks. These could survive on grain and their performance would be enhanced by scraps, which would produce a few eggs and the occasional carcass. However, you would still have to find some high protein feed for the chicks you hatch or they won't grow very well.

We buy feed when we need it, avoid feeding more mouths than we have to, and use waste as much as we can. That is our compromise.

THE LEGAL IMPACTS

As already indicated, the fourth major issue is the law, because it has an impact on several major areas of livestock keeping. They are:

- killing;
- sales of meat;
- disposal of waste including dead animals;
- animal movements;
- feed.

Killing

There are no restrictions on killing small quantities of poultry and rabbits at home. Larger livestock may be killed at home for the consumption of the farmer himself. Cows, sheep and goats have an additional set of rules about removing the brain and spinal cord to avoid transmission of BSE and scrapie to humans. After establishing this, the water gets much muddier.

There are several advantages to home killing: the animals don't have to travel and are less stressed; and you will get all your own offal and trotters back. Normally these are all thrown in a bin and not offered back to you; if you do get a piece of liver it will probably not be from your animals.

At the time of writing the rules are unclear. Home killing is certainly perfectly legal, but until DEFRA sorts out its rules it appears that you, the farmer, will have to eat it all yourself without passing any to the rest of your family. Further, anyone you engage to advise you can do only that: advise you. They cannot help you physically, even though they know better than you how to do it properly.

Sales of Meat

You can sell your surplus poultry and rabbits, but you may not sell any larger animals that have been killed or cut at home. You may sell meat prepared by a butcher, but be sure that it goes straight from freezer to freezer.

The Disposal of Waste

The disposal of waste products (guts and bones) creates another set of problems. You certainly cannot bury them in any place where they will pollute a water course. Farmers are not allowed to bury anything at all, and subscribe to the 'Fallen Stock Scheme', which would also take guts. If you are keeping just rabbits and hens the rules that apply to farmers don't apply to you, as you are not a farmer. However, once you progress to keeping cloven-footed animals you will have to register your holding with DEFRA and will be given a holding number. Are you now a farmer for the purposes of this legislation? Nor can I fertilize my vegetable garden

THE CONTROL OF VERMIN

However carefully the feed for the animals or the produce for your own consumption is stored, some will spill and vermin will be attracted. Traps for mice and rats should be kept baited at all times, and when the traps indicate that vermin are about, poison should also be put down. In particular at harvest time enormous numbers of rats and mice leave the fields for the comfort of your rabbitries and feed sheds, and if not controlled they will do serious damage to your buildings, as well as to relations with your neighbours. The day your farmer neighbour gets out his combine harvester, set all the traps and put out poison. Do not wait.

If our furry friends move in, it is a good idea to check to see if your local council still has a rat man. He may be free or subsidized, and does have some experience of these things. These people will not normally come out for precautionary baiting but are definitely there for you when the pests are in residence. If not, there are always commercial firms to back up your defences.

Many ways of simplifying life involve using feed hoppers. If vermin are about the hoppers will have to be taken out at night so they will eat the poisoned corn; there is no value in giving them choice!

Take care with poisons; I know it is obvious, but a reminder never hurts.

with these parts, which seems absurd when the alternative is to go out and buy blood, fish and bonemeal, made in part from abattoir wastes.

There are two major sources of information that you can refer to for further details: the DEFRA website and your local Trading Standards office. At the time of writing DEFRA have withdrawn various rules for reconsideration. When you plan to kill, the best advice is to see what the websites are currently saying, and to ring the local Trading Standards office, whose personnel we have always found very helpful.

If you are lucky enough still to have a local knackerman he will take away a bag of bits for a few pounds.

Animal Movements

Restrictions on animal movements apply to all mammals with cloven hooves. For all practical purposes that is pigs, goats, sheep and cows. The basic rules are that you will need a holding number which you get by registering with the Rural Payments Agency. Then you will need to keep a book to record all movements on to and off your premises; the book will periodically be inspected. In addition there are 'standstill' periods after stock has been moved on to your land when no stock may move off unless for slaughter.

Rules Concerning Feed

The last set of rules concern feed. You may not feed waste meat to animals. I don't think that stops you feeding some meat waste to poultry, but there is a limit to how much they can clear up. There is an absolute prohibition on catering waste being fed to pigs – and this is a shame, because that was what pigs were originally bred for; however, the swine fever and foot-and-mouth epidemics have both been caused by this practice.

It is amazing how often we see different species keeping one another company.

You can feed garden waste freely. The detailed rules for all these issues are available from the DEFRA website. You should not keep any stock without prior reference to that site, and you will need to review it periodically for changes. This is not just a bureaucratic exercise: imagine how you would feel as a small producer if you were the source of a major disease outbreak.

HEALTH AND MEDICATION

You will rarely need medicines for your own stock if they are kept well. As a basic first aid kit you should at least have some 'purple spray' available for all cuts and infections: this is a general purpose antiseptic spray supplied by feed and agricultural merchants. Things do go wrong however, and the worst source of this is when you bring new stock in, which can bring parasites and disease with them, and it can spread to your stock.

Keep a close eye on all livestock. If they seem less glossy or active than usual they may need treatment. Look particularly at backsides and feet. Backsides should be clean. For poultry and sheep it may be necessary to clip off caked filth with sharp scissors or shears. If they still don't look

right this may indicate digestive problems.

Cloven feet need maintenance. They must be trimmed from time to time, cleaned out and then sprayed with purple if there is any damage.

For a beginner the answer to all these needs is to call a vet. Get a proper farm vet (not a pet specialist), and use them as a source of your personal training. They, and indeed other keepers, can show how to trim feet and administer injections; in time you will be able to treat most conditions yourself. Drugs are available from vets, though once you have a holding number you may also be able to purchase them on line.

DO NOT OVER-COMMIT

We move into another level of commitment with livestock. If animals cannot be fed and watered regularly (usually twice a day, every day) then don't keep them. There are automatic feeding and watering systems available and many of them are very good, but even then it is essential at the very least to walk past them to check everything is in order, and at some stage the home-produced feed must be fed to the animals or we are factory farmers too.

But if you can commit, get on and enjoy your livestock. They will be a pleasure.

CHAPTER 10

Rabbits

There can be few meat-producing animals that are as productive as the rabbit. In theory the breeding capability of the rabbit is spectacular: does have a thirty-one day gestation period, and can be mated the day after they 'kindle' (give birth), which means that in one year each doe could produce 11.7 litters. If each of those litters has ten young in it, then each doe could produce 117 young rabbits a year.

In practice it is not quite so impressive, and on the garden scale we need not push the frontiers quite so hard. Rabbits are, though, the single best starting point for domestic meat production. They grow quickly, giving a decent carcass in anything from eight to sixteen weeks from birth (they could take longer, but they will breed at about eighteen weeks and the sexes will need to be separated before then if they have not been put in the freezer first). Rabbits are also particularly good users of scraps and waste. They are flexible users of vegetable garden produce, and can benefit from wild food. Finally, they are easy to kill and prepare.

Unlike other stock in this book there is a real advantage in terms of flavour if you can get your youngsters to grow reasonably fast. If they grow too slowly they taste more like wild rabbit, and fail to be the really exciting culinary treat that rabbit can be. Wild rabbit can be quite strong in flavour and needs salting to be edible; good domestic rabbit tastes similar to, but rather better than, turkey. To achieve this fast-growing, well flavoured animal means feeding it well (including some protein), and selecting your stock with care.

Start small and buy one or two does, and either buy a buck or find a friend whose buck you can use. Then decide when you wish to produce rabbits. We like to have a steady production throughout the year, so for us this is one litter every two or three months. There are, though, parts of the year, especially between February and April, when food is not that plentiful from the garden, and for the first year of rabbit keeping it is probably a good idea to rest does then. If you breed too energetically you will have a problem housing all the youngsters anyway. Assume that a doe will produce around twenty-five young a year (less than half that of the very best commercial flocks, but many of the latter achieve less than they should, with very high levels of mortality), do the arithmetic, and start making or acquiring the hutches.

HOUSING

Assume that you will be buying large rabbits, and do not be tempted by small hutches; breeding does in particular

Is there a better way to use pea pods? I'm not convinced that
pea pod burgundy was ever really a runner.

should have plenty of space. When they have young running about and large amounts of food in the pen for them all to eat, it can get quite cramped, and they still need a corner they can use as a lavatory without fouling their food. Give a breeding doe at least two-thirds of a square metre (yard) of floor, and a pen height of half a metre (about 2ft); more will do no harm. The bucks and young-stock that you will be retaining for future breeding need about half a square metre and a pen half a metre in height. You will also need hutches for fatteners, and we like to allow space on the basis of no more than six rabbits per square metre. The more space the better, as you can clean out less often.

Construction techniques are many and varied. The main points to ensure are that access for cleaning is good, draughts are minimized, and an area of relative privacy provided (usually a nestbox) for breeding does. Suggested structures involve building multi-storey hutches simply because they take up less space and materials; two or three high are both acceptable. Don't, however, let the floors leak on to stock below!

In theory, at least, I don't like wire cages such as those used commercially, but it has to be admitted that a great many rabbits are housed and bred in them with very good results. These cages are cheap and easy to assemble, particularly as wood is becoming increasingly expensive. On the other hand, good wooden hutches seem somehow more comfortable, although a few authorities state that wood absorbs too much moisture, that it allows ammonia to build up, and finally rots. To be safe, treat the wood well before the hutches are occupied, and use a little sawdust under the straw bedding to absorb any excess moisture – though not too much as it can affect babies' eyes.

Cages should be sited in a well ventilated shed, but hutches can be inside or outside in a sheltered place, perhaps against a wall or stout fence (rabbits will eat their way through ordinary fence panels in no time at all). If outside, provide weather protection with a good overhang on the roof, and extra shelter in really bad conditions. There are some advantages of a shed over an outside site if only because mucking out in bad weather is less uncomfortable than outside; but a shed must not be used if it gets too hot or if the air cannot be kept fresh. The design of your accommodation will be dictated as much by the site and availability of buildings as by any other factor.

Give nestboxes to pregnant does at least a week before they are due, or if using wooden structures make them a permanent part of the hutch. When settled with you, some will happily use a corner of the hutch without any special provision.

Bedding should be mainly straw; the sawdust beneath maximizes mucking out intervals. Barley straw is preferable to wheat straw as the rabbits tend to eat a bit of it, but either will do. Shake it out well – a slice from a bale unshaken is really not much use – and keep it topped up so there is a comfortable-looking layer in the pens. Before does are due to kindle, give them a little extra and they will pile it up into a bed. Clean out once a week into the hens' deep-litter yards or on to the muck heap. Another advantage of wire cages is that litter except for nest building is not required and mucking out is less frequent: obviously a consideration to balance against the aesthetic argument.

A simple nestbox.

Alternative Accommodation

It is possible to build moveable 'arks' in which to house your rabbits. The advantage is that you are taking the rabbits to the green food rather than the food to the rabbits. The system was originally introduced by one Captain Morant, and they are generally known as Morant arks. Arks are usually constructed from wood and wire netting. They can be whatever size you like as long as they can be moved easily, and must have a sheltered area, with a floor, of about the same size as any other hutch. Wire the floors as well as the sides or they will dig their way out. Arks are not ideal breeding accommodation.

The disadvantages of arks are that you can only use them for part of the year; the rest of the time they are cluttering up good storage space, they cost too much for their benefit, and they do not protect stock from eating poisonous weeds.

The colony system for keeping rabbits is now very little used. There were two types: the extensive outdoor warrens that probably started in the Middle Ages and which are not within the scope of this book because they take up too much space; and the small indoor warren in a shed or barn. This latter is still quite possible and has in the last few years become our favourite. Using a shed or loosebox made secure against dogs, foxes and other intruders, all that will be required within the building are nestboxes for the does and a separate hutch for the buck.

This system has definite advantages:

- The rabbits seem much calmer and happier; this equates to growing better.
- Labour is reduced considerably by using feed hoppers and drinkers, which can be made to last all week (providing you can control rats).
- It is much easier to feed branches and other large pieces of greenstuff, which do not have to be cut up.
- Mucking out is less frequent.

The secret is to start with does that get on well together; sisters are ideal. Take them to the buck on the same day (or over a few days if there are too many of them), provide nestboxes – and wait. Eight weeks after birth take the does back to the bucks and clear the offspring to separate accommodation or the freezer by twelve weeks, when the next lot should be born. The results for us have been very good, and the system has saved much work.

A further use of sheds is to keep all the does in one shed and remove them to hutches for breeding, and then to use sheds or hutches for fattening the young rabbits after weaning. You will need to keep tabs on the does to know when they are due to give birth (or 'kindle'). Don't worry that sheds are dark, as rabbits really don't care; they must, though, have adequate ventilation in order to avoid ammonia build-up from rotting litter.

BUYING STOCK

The selection of stock is important, especially when you begin. Many of the traditional meat breeds have been taken over for so long by 'the fancy' that growth rates are just not good enough. Commercial stock is available both as improved strains of some of the traditional breeds, usually New Zealand Whites and Californians, and as hybrids.

There is some virtue in breeding rabbits together from two varieties giving, usually, slightly better results as a result of 'hybrid vigour'. Traditionally there were some well known crosses used, perhaps the most famous being the Flemish Giant buck with a Belgian Hare or an English doe (to avoid confusion, the Belgian Hare is indeed a rabbit), also the New Zealand White and the Californian.

Once again, though, there can be some better meat characteristics in some of the old breeds over the improved strains. This flavour difference is less noticeable in rabbits than the meat texture, which ranges from fine to quite coarse, and I would suggest that you experiment. Certainly using largely commercial stock will give the best growth rates. We keep a range of varieties, and our current favourite is to cross Rex rabbits with a variety of other types. Some pet sales help to pay for the feed, and Rex offspring are particularly attractive as pets because of their very fine coats.

Learn to handle rabbits carefully. Yes, it is quite correct to catch them by their ears and they can be lifted that way too, but do get a hand under them to support them and to control their back legs as quickly as you can. Frequent handling is not essential, but it does make for more pleasant creatures. Beware when returning them to their hutches as they will 'kick for home' as soon as they see it. Put them in backwards, and you will save untold scratches.

A word about sexing rabbits (and the correct assessment of gender really does help). At the adult stage a fairly cursory inspection will reveal the presence or otherwise of balls. Nipples are also fairly clearly defined for does. To sex younger rabbits it is necessary to hold them and carefully expose their organ by applying light pressure to both sides of the vent. In the bucks the opening is circular and in the does it is V-shaped. Do be careful with them, as you can damage them doing this too roughly; they usually manage to scratch you quite effectively, too.

Teeth and Claws

If your rabbit grows very long teeth it will not do well. It is possible to trim them (with side cutters) but it is a fault and it is better to replace the rabbit. Do not breed replacement stock from it. Feed brassica stems and twigs – for example apple prunings – to give all rabbits something to work their teeth on; otherwise they will eat the hutch.

Rabbits confined to hutches may grow very long claws. It is advisable to trim them with a pair of side cutters periodically. Do not cut off too much or they will bleed; look for the point where the colour of the claw changes, and cut back only to that.

FEEDING

Despite a general feeling that stock in the garden farm need not be pushed to commercial levels of productivity, the best rabbit carcasses are from young animals that have grown fast. Our target is a rabbit weighing in (live) at about 2kg (4½lb) when it is twelve weeks old. That target is not easy, and even if they weigh only half that, they should be killed by sixteen weeks old at the latest (commercially they are achieving killing weight at eight weeks old).

If at all possible start out from the assumption that at least some of the rabbit's diet will be home produced. They eat green foods in preference to anything else that you can give them. It goes without saying that vegetable trimmings of anything we eat should be offered to the rabbits, but a few crops should be considered specifically for them. Particular favourites are lucerne (alfalfa), which gives a superb volume of high quality feed, vetches, chicories and Jerusalem artichokes, all of which are referred to in detail in the growing sections of this book.

In addition to home-produced feed you will need some bought stuff, both because home-produced will not always be available, and because the bought stuff is quick and easy to feed it when time is short. Unfortunately most of the rabbit food easily available comes from pet shops. Despite the fact that the best of these foods are now quite low in terms of additives and therefore appear an acceptable compromise, they fail on their protein content, which is usually about 14 per cent against a protein requirement of about 18 per cent to get the level of growth that we are aiming for; 14 per cent is quite enough for a pet, but our rabbits work and need more than that (except perhaps the bucks, who must be watched to ensure they don't get fat).

It is possible to use these low protein feeds and to supplement them with other protein. With care and experience, milk (cow's or goat's), soya and other ingredients could be blended in the ration, but feed (especially the milk) would have to be kept fresh at all times. To get it right you would need to be fairly skilful, and time is better spent tracking down better feed. Several mills produce commercial rabbit feeds of 18 per cent protein, but they are all aiming at major units that require growth promoters and other additives. However, these mills also produce additive-free feed to the same sort of specification for use in the last week before killing (they say this keeps the additives out of the human food chain), and this is what we need. One other convenient factor with rabbits is that food comes in bags, not in bulk, as bulk handling breaks the pellets into dust which they cannot eat.

In general, because rabbits will always eat good green food in preference to anything else, it is not wasteful to give hay and concentrates ad lib as well. Given these to turn to if they need them, rabbits will generally balance their own diet and not be forced by hunger to eat anything that is not good for them. That gives you the freedom to experiment a little with the green food that you grow both for them and for yourself.

If all you feed your rabbits comes out of a bag, you will need between 3 and 4kg (7 and 9lb) of feed for every kilo of young animal produced according to the quality of the stock. Since you will be mixing it with green stuff where you cannot easily measure the dry-matter content, this may seem an irrelevant statistic. However, if

you do calculate how much you would have had to buy on this basis and compare with your actual purchases, the real value of home-produced feed is apparent. One good reason for not having too many rabbits is that as the numbers increase, an increasing proportion of the feed has to be bought in. A balance must be struck.

Keep vessels clean and water fresh; that way disease is much less likely. With all livestock an occasional piece of fresh garlic in the water can help general health.

Hedge clippings must be used with some care, but if the rabbits are not too hungry, most of the poisonous stuff just gets ignored anyway and as a rough rule of thumb if it is deciduous, it is worth a try (although I'll tell you now they will not eat elder). The only exception is ivy, which despite being evergreen is edible to rabbits except in summer when in flower. It should be saved for the winter anyway when other food is scarcer.

Weeds, too, have their place. Most small weeds from gardening are probably best fed to the hens as they usually get too muddy, but if allowed to grow larger (well, we all have holidays sometimes) many are good rabbit food. They include coltsfoot, comfrey, chickweed, cow parsley, dock, fat hen, plantain, sow thistles and watercress. Groundsel is much loved by rabbits and better fed to them than left lying around. As a weed it requires careful control. Left on the path after being pulled it will nearly always manage to produce seed before dying.

BREEDING

A rabbit's breeding age is from about five months for does and six months for bucks.

Feed Month by Month from the Garden Farm

January	Broccoli, Brussels sprout plants when finished, blown sprouts and outer leaves, cabbage, cauliflower, celery, chicories, fodder beet, Jerusalem artichoke tubers, kale, parsley, potatoes, parsnips and leeks (cooked), spinach beet, swede.
February	Broccoli, brussels sprout plants when finished, blown sprouts and outer leaves, cabbage, cauliflower, celery, chicories, fodder beet, jerusalem artichoke tubers, kale, parsley, potatoes, parsnips & leeks (cooked), spinach beet.
March	Broccoli, Brussels sprout plants when finished, blown sprouts and outer leaves, cabbage, cauliflower, celery, chicories, Jerusalem artichoke tubers, kale, parsley, potatoes, parsnips and leeks (cooked), spinach beet.
April	Broccoli, Brussels sprout plants when finished, blown sprouts and outer leaves, cabbage, cauliflower, chicories, kale, parsley, potatoes, parsnips and leeks (cooked), spinach beet.
May	Cauliflower, chicories, hedge clippings particularly hawthorn, kale, lucerne, parsley, spinach beet, spring cabbage.
June	Cabbage, carrots, cauliflower, chicories, hedge clippings particularly hawthorn, lettuce, lucerne, parsley, spinach beet, strawberry runners, turnip, willow.
July	Beetroot, cabbage, carrots, cauliflower, chicories, hedge clippings particularly hawthorn, lettuce, lucerne, parsley, pea pods and haulm, spinach beet, strawberry runners, turnip, willow.
August	Beetroot, cabbage, carrots, cauliflower, chicories, lettuce, lucerne, parsley, pea pods and haulm, spinach beet, strawberry runners, sweetcorn plants, turnip.
September	Beetroot, broccoli, cabbage, carrots, cauliflower, chicories, Jerusalem artichoke tops if necessary (at the expense of some tuber development), kohlrabi, lettuce, lucerne, parsley, spinach beet, swede, sweetcorn plants as soon as the harvest is finished, turnip.
October	Beetroot, broccoli, cabbage, carrots, cauliflower, chicories, Jerusalem artichoke tops, kohlrabi, lettuce, parsley, spinach beet, swede.
November	Cabbage, carrots (now from store), cauliflower, celery, chicories, Jerusalem artichoke tubers, kale, lettuce, parsley, potatoes, parsnips and leeks (cooked), spinach beet, swede.
December	Cabbage, carrots (now from store), cauliflower, celery, chicories, Jerusalem artichoke tubers, kale, lettuce, parsley, potatoes, parsnips and leeks (cooked), spinach beet, swede.

ROUTINES

Although not really possible for the larger stock, it is possible to cheat a bit with rabbits and poultry. Feed and water them with automatic or high capacity feeders and drinkers, and for at least one of the daily visits have just a quick look round. You will need to bring your domestic scraps to them once a day and probably some home-grown food, but otherwise as long as they have pellets and water they will not come to any harm.

Even if our ambition is to avoid feeding too much in the way of 'bag food' (and I think that is too ambitious anyway), you must always have plenty in stock. There will always be a grim January day when the sky is made of lead, the car is giving you trouble and the whole family has a cold, when you need an easy option rather than going foraging for animal food. We aim, of course, to give animals as much fresh greenstuff as we can, but in the middle of winter it will rarely be their main meal.

Similarly we do not wish to waste the home-produced food that we do have, and would wish for it all to be used up effectively. Probably in the worst weeks of the year you will feed bought-in rations for the working days, and the home-produced roots and greenstuffs can be fed at the weekends only. In summer we would see that as failure, in winter that has to be acceptable.

Old books talk about breeding age being anything up to ten months for larger breeds. Assuming your stock is of modern varieties, perhaps the five-month rule will do, but for older types do not rush them: you will be the loser in the end if the animal never reaches its peak both in its own performance and that of the offspring.

Mating

When the doe is old enough she can make her first visit to the buck for mating. The doe must always be taken to the buck rather than the other way round, unless you want your buck attacked by the doe. If all goes well the buck will approach the doe, which will stand for him to mount her. He will fall off with a satisfied grunt a few seconds later and the job is done. Make a note of the date, add thirty days, and wait for action.

Life is not often quite that simple, especially with some individual rabbits. Does are often reluctant to mate, and after running around for a moment or two they stick their backsides in a corner and refuse to co-operate. If this happens, take them out and try again the next day, which very often solves the problem. Two green foods are notable for helping to encourage shy does: they are parsley and groundsel, and should be fed generously until the problem is resolved. In our experience they have always worked. As a last resort accommodate the doe in a cage previously occupied by a buck (not cleaned out), and see if the pheromones will get her going.

If the buck does not want to perform he is not healthy (probably dying, knowing rabbits) so ensure that his food and conditions are the best, give him a rest, and use another one.

Kindling

Keep an eye on the dates. A week before the doe is due, put a nestbox in the hutch in the most private clean corner, and make sure she has some clean straw to carry into the nest. Nestboxes should be a lidless box about 40 x 30cm (16 x 12in), with three sides about 25cm (10in) high, with a hole or simply a small step on the fourth side for access. Make sure she has a little extra straw in the two days before the litter is due. Try not to muck out for the next few days. If all goes well a mound of straw and fur will appear, and shortly after it will fill with youngsters.

Rabbits are shy, especially at this stage, and there is no advantage in interfering until the young are at least twenty-four hours old. At that point a gentle hand in the nest can count the result and remove any dead ones. Occasionally the doe puts the young in two groups and they should gently be put in one. We find that the average is around six or seven with eight at best, and since does normally only have eight nipples, more than eight young seems excessive (having said that, we have had does regularly rearing ten). If litters do get too big you may be unable to do anything except give the doe as much good food as you can and hope for the best, though it is possible to foster on to another doe if she has kindled either at the same time or in the previous two days.

Fostering (some call it adoption, but I doubt the due legal processes are followed) is quite easy if you have two does that have kindled within a day or so of each other. Take both does out of their hutches, take the excess of the big litter and mix them up together with the young of the other litter for long enough for them to all smell the same, and then put the does back. Usually it works without a hitch.

Weaning

We then have to decide when to wean the young from their mother. There are no absolute rules for this, and the more commercial units have to wean at four weeks old because the does kindle again only a few days after, having been mated again as soon as the litter was born. On our smaller scale, replacing does frequently because they are worn out means we would need additional pens to rear replacements in, and also quickly introduces the risk of inbreeding unless the bucks, too, are changed regularly.

We prefer to treat the does more gently. An old standard practice is to wean at eight weeks or two months, and this means that if the doe is mated immediately after weaning she will be on a three-month cycle between litters. It is worth stressing that the doe should go to the buck immediately after weaning, as the chances of a successful mating do fall away if she is allowed to rest.

False Pregnancy

Perhaps a quick word is appropriate on the subject of false pregnancy, which does occasionally happen. The symptoms are easy to spot, as the doe makes her nest between ten and fourteen days early without giving birth to anything. Take her back to the buck and start again, and that is usually all that is required. In my experience this is more likely to happen to first-timers and new stock; if it happens to your established does, give them a bit more attention and make sure they are in generally good condition.

The Commercial Breeder

Talking to a rabbit farmer, I found an interesting example of the differences between commercial production and our own. We hardly ever have any rabbits die except when we kill them, yet for him, a major problem is mortality of his stock: he loses rabbits right through from the time the litter is born until the young rabbits are ready. He was saying that in most commercial flocks probably 25 per cent of the young born don't live to market age, and in some flocks the percentage is higher. There is a sign on his wall that says 'Rabbits are Born with an Ambition to Die'. However, he is simply wrong, and the fact is that he works the does too hard. It may make commercial sense to him, but it makes no sense at all to me.

HARVESTING

Rabbits are killed easily with a sharp blow on the back of the neck or top of the head. Do not try to wring their necks unless you are very strong and experienced: if you get it wrong it can hurt you as well as the rabbit; when stretched full length rabbits are longer than you expect, and the fatal twist risks damaging an arm muscle leaving the rabbit alive and you in agony.

Take the rabbit by its hind legs and let it hang; it will quickly do so without making a fuss (if you are right-handed hold it in your left hand). If its ears hang forwards it should be hit hard once just below the ears with a blunt instrument; if it holds the ears up, hit the top of the head; either way the area adjacent to the ears is the target. As for the blunt instrument, we find a broken fork handle or dibber about the right size and weight, but other tools would do equally well. If you wish to bleed it, stick it just behind the ears with a knife and hold it until the blood stops. We don't bother with this, we merely hang it up to

let the blood run to the head, which is cut off in due course; however, if you were to sell the rabbit skinned, head and all, it would be essential.

The rabbit will kick several times after death, which is due entirely to muscular contractions and not to any pain being endured by the rabbit.

Paunching and Skinning

The rabbit must now be paunched: this is the term for removing its guts (strictly stomach, intestine and gall bladder). Cut off a small piece of fur in the centre of the stomach. With a very sharp knife slit the belly from just in front of the vent to where the ribs join the breast bone; hold the knife very carefully to ensure that the guts will not puncture. Generally we hold them up by the back legs again at this stage and try to identify the bladder. Having found it, pinch just below the base and pull it clear of the carcass. The remaining contents will fall out fairly easily, any reluctant bits being eased out carefully. Put the rabbit on its back and split the bone to release the end of the intestine as it reaches the vent. Cut away the vent itself.

Leave the heart, liver and kidneys if you want it to look like something in a French butcher's shop, otherwise take them out, too. If you wish to use the livers for pâté or gravy it is necessary to remove the gall bladder. Again, pinch and pull; but if the gall bladder bursts, the affected liver will have to be thrown away.

To skin rabbits, start by removing the feet at the first joint up the leg with a sharp knife. Then, from the hole already there, separate the skin from the flesh – which is surprisingly easy (hence the term 'skin a rabbit', traditionally used when undressing children). Insert a finger or thumb between the flesh and the skin and work backwards to one hind leg. Once the thigh is free of the skin, the leg can be pulled through and will tear around the ankle. Next do the other back leg. Cut the tail away from the body, and with one pull the skin will pull right up to the front legs. Do them as you did the back ones, and pull again to bring the skin up to the head. It is possible to skin the head, but in the spirit of an easy life we just cut the head off and throw it and the skin away. Pelts can be kept, cured and made into wonderful coats, but we don't have that much time. If you want, put them (minus the heads) in the freezer; you may get the time to do a job on a decent quantity one day.

The next part is not too demanding: just let the meat 'set'. This means leaving the carcass in a cool place for at least four hours, otherwise the meat will be tough. Your meal is now ready to cook.

There is a certain amount of waste from all skinning and gutting operations. In the previous chapter I referred to problems of disposal of this. Assuming you interpret the rules as I do, fertilize the garden with it. Ensure that your vegetable garden has a bed free in which you can bury this waste two spits down. It is a very good fertilizer, part of our original cycle of virtue, but must be put out of the reach of digging dogs.

If all this is too much for you, many butchers will do the job for you for a modest fee.

CHAPTER 11

Poultry

HENS

A few hens on the domestic scale are almost essential. They produce the best muck we can get, they eat scraps and weeds that nothing else can manage (often just because it is dirty or half rotten), and produce eggs and a few carcasses for meat. On the other hand, if you keep too many they will become an expense and waste food will not be a major part of their diet. Also, all poultry require more preparation for the table than the rabbit, and the breeding process, whether with broody hens or incubators, needs more input from you at every stage of the process than the rabbits that manage so well by themselves.

Work on the premise of one adult hen for each member of the family, unless you are major egg eaters. Keep a cockerel if you can, as he will keep them all in order and enable you to breed a small number every year to replace stock as it gets old. The by-product of this will be a couple of carcasses and the pleasure of chicks hatching in the spring, which few are so cynical not to find an uplifting experience.

Varieties

Hens come in so many shapes and sizes that it is very hard to lay down too many rules. To start with there are full-sized fowls and there are bantams. Basically, bantams are bred simply to be smaller, so they will lay fewer eggs, the eggs will be smaller but the birds will eat less. Nevertheless some varieties of bantam do lay very well indeed (probably the best is the Ancona) and some large fowls lay very badly (the list is long). Moreover good layers often make poor broody hens.

Our solution is to run a few bantams together with a trio of larger fowls. The larger fowls produce more eggs and the bantams hatch a clutch for us every year. Ideal bantams for this purpose are crossed with a strange but very broody bird, the silkie; these 'silkie crosses' are widely available and valued by pheasant hatchers, amongst others.

As for large bird varieties, either try commercial hybrids for maximum performance, or choose a traditional breed which you may find more interesting. There is a huge range of these traditional breeds to choose from. Beware of those breeds whose only merit is on the show table of fancy fowl lovers, and select from one of the 'utility' breeds bred for eggs or meat. We have kept Leghorns, which proved to be prolific white egg layers; Rhode Island Reds and Light Sussex which give decent eggs and a larger carcass; or Welsummers for brown eggs. Marans are also widely used for brown eggs, but I don't like them much as they can be quite

A silkie with chicks.

aggressive in the hen house and I prefer a more tranquil life. Others that we have tried include Speckled Sussex, but they did not really excel, Dorkings which are lovely but not very prolific, Legbars which are scatty and in my opinion not a real breed anyway, Barnevelders, beautiful birds and very dark brown eggs but poor performers, and a wide range of bantams, many of which are thrifty and produce quite well though the carcasses are inevitably rather small.

Commercial hens are all now hybrids, derived by crossing two carefully selected bloodlines, and most are designed for intensive systems; however, there are also quite a few hybrid types designed for less intensive systems. Some of these we have tried and they have done very well for us.

Obviously fertile eggs will not be produced without a cockerel. A cockerel is also very useful for maintaining harmony amongst the flock, and without one it is very difficult to introduce new birds to the hen house. Even bringing in youngstock that you have bred on the premises to mix with the main flock runs the risk of fighting and bloodshed. If possible it is best to run

**Cockerels can be very pretty, too. This one is an
Exchequer Leghorn.**

a cockerel with the hens at all times, and a good one should keep all sizes of bird in order. Where neighbour concerns (or your own fears of sleep deprivation) prevent you having one, then try at least to negotiate the loan of one for the first week after mixing strange birds together.

Housing

Sadly the days of allowing a few hens to scratch around the yard are almost gone. This is nothing to do with bureaucratic interference or damage to the neighbours' gardens (although that may be an issue) – it is because of the enormous numbers of foxes now at large. Unless you are prepared to take a gun and attack the local population, risking the wrath of hunters for stealing their sport and of the anti-hunters for destroying their anthropomorphic icons, you will have to house hens, and indeed other poultry, to protect them from the fox.

All sorts of housing can be used, but first you have to decide what access they should have to the outside. We have lost too many to foxes and ours are now accommodated in a bought multi-storey henhouse. The joy of this particular design is that the hens are moved once a week and this gives them access to fresh grass, which improves egg quality and general health enormously.

Our other system is to use a building where part of at least one wall is made of wire mesh, taking care that the hens have shade as well as light and fresh air. Within this shed we keep the birds on 'deep litter'. These words conjure up visions of vast sheds full of birds that never see the light of day living on a bed of their own excrement. It need not be like that. Earlier on, when talking about muck, I said that the bedding for these hens is often second-hand, having once been used by the rabbits or goats. This gives them a considerable amount of interesting material to scratch through. Add to that a bucket or two full of weeds when gardening, and our birds seem happy to scratch around for hours every day. That is, after all, what hens do, and it seems to be a very good system. Every few weeks it pays to take a fork into the hen house and turn the litter over; this stops it getting solid and frees up sprouted grains and a few insects as a treat for the birds. I still prefer, though, to let the hens out in the sunshine whenever possible.

When using this system, bear in mind that hens scratch quite energetically and their water will fill with muck quite quickly. Try putting it on a block or in some other place where it will keep reasonably clean.

The muck produced from this system can be cleared and used directly on the ground, or worked through the compost bins. It is very good for making compost bins work well because it is an 'activator'; by the time the hens have worked it for a few weeks even the straw is broken into small pieces, and, mixed with two contributions of animal manure where you are using second-hand straw, it really is fairly potent stuff – as a fertilizer probably as good as you can get organically.

Outside straw or deep-litter yards also work well, but in wet conditions the fork is even more important. All outside runs will have to have fences nearly 2m (5ft) high, and even then a capping is a good idea to prevent foxes climbing. Care must also be taken not to give foxes any jumping off points.

Whatever your hens' accommodation, they require a perch. Hens must roost at night, and they need enough perching space not only to do that, but also to fly up to their place without knocking their

A perfectly decent house and run for a few birds.

neighbours off their perches. Allow about 30cm (12in) of perch length each for bantams, and 50cm (20in) for full-sized fowls – but the more the merrier, and then they can choose for their own best comfort and, therefore, performance. The birds like them as high as possible, but don't expect them to fly up more than a metre or so without an interim perch on the way. Modern birds are bred for egg laying rather than flying.

Another requirement is a dust bath. Some old bonfire ashes or similar are good for this, in a box large enough for a hen to get herself smothered in ash and unsettle any parasites that might otherwise be wanting to move in. All birds like a bath of some sort; think of the bird baths in our gardens. For hens the best ones are dust.

If the plan is for these birds to lay eggs for you, nestboxes must be provided. If the hens are kept in a shed or other building into which you can walk without bending double, they need be no more than a box with an open front. The box should be a 40cm (16in) cube for large fowls, and 30cm (12in) for bantams. Fit a lip to the bottom of the open front of about 10cm (4in) to retain a little straw or hay. Nestboxes should be off the ground but lower than the perches, otherwise the birds will sleep (and crap) in them; if more than 50cm (20in) off the ground a low perch should be supplied to help them up there.

If you need access to nestboxes from outside the building, take a look at proprietary poultry arks and their nestboxes with external access lids. Some of the boxes should have china eggs (literally that) in them just to remind the hens where to lay (golf balls are just as good). They also serve to encourage broodies (*see* The Broody Hen below) to 'stick' before setting them on real eggs.

Daily concentration in the nestbox.

Keep the nestboxes clean, and the eggs should also be clean. There is no serious risk from dirty eggs and they can be washed, but clean eggs are nicer.

FEEDING

Good laying poultry can't maintain their performance without a high protein ration. About 16 per cent of their food needs to be protein. The amount of 'bought-in' protein that you require for hens will depend on how much food they are finding, or being given in the form of scraps, and although we have a lot of scraps from rather wasteful children, we still find that some additional protein helps.

If it were not for the hens we should be angrier about wasted meat, cheese and other wonderful hen food. The best strategy is to save all scraps for the morning feed, with some pellets fed, too.

In the evenings feed grain, preferably reasonable quality wheat. Grain takes a long while to digest in their crops, keeping their digestive system busy for as long as possible through the hours of darkness. One point to remember is to feed the evening feed well before dark so that they can fill those crops before going to roost, which they will do when the sun tells them to, whether or not they have eaten enough.

Pellets can now be bought both as additive free and organic, and it is worth finding suppliers to suit your preferences. Needless to say organic is quite a lot more expensive.

Aim to feed sufficient in the morning so that small amounts are left which the hens can scratch over all day; in the evening feed only as much as they eat in 20min. Food left lying around longer than this, especially overnight, only attracts rats. Hoppers can be used but they should be hung high enough off the ground to make sure the rats cannot help themselves; but do make sure that the hens can. For us, the rats have learned where the food is, and they will always find a way of getting to the hoppers so we only use them when we are away.

Rats are a real problem. Watch out for their elongated droppings, and if you see them, change your feeding regime as you are certainly feeding them, too. Be prepared to trap or poison them regularly.

All poultry also require grit, first to use in their gizzard in the grinding process that passes for their digestion, and secondly to extract calcium from it to make egg shells. The first is available to any bird that can scratch the soil, but otherwise should be provided, and the second must always be given. The usual form is oystershell for shell manufacture, although some people bake old egg shells instead; for me, this cycle of feeding back animal produce to the same species is to be avoided. If the birds are inside, a mixture of grit for both purposes is available as 'mixed grit' or 'poultry grit'.

A word, too, about water. Clean water must be available to all stock all of the time – and clean means clean. Get your hands dirty and scrub vessels whenever necessary. As mentioned before, a small piece of garlic in the water can, some say, act as a tonic. If that doesn't keep everyone fit, you might try a few drops of cider vinegar in the water; some swear by it.

THE BROODY HEN

The 'broody' deserves her own section. This most noble and useful creature can be used to hatch and rear for you replacements for your flock: ducks, geese, guinea fowl, pheasants, partridge and more. With a few general words to you on management she can be left pretty much to her own devices, and she will certainly be less work than a mechanical incubator and brooder. She will also provide excitement for the children (and adults).

The best broody hens are not your best laying birds; in fact good laying birds are unreliable as broodies, and if you have a choice, they should be avoided. The very best are a cross between a 'silkie', which is a strange, fluffy sort of hen, and one of the bantam breeds. Traditional gamekeepers would take a lot of care over breeding these.

One day late in March or perhaps early in April you will find that one of the hens takes even longer than usual to lay an egg. You will give her a little longer just to make sure and then go back and lift her off to see what is happening. Probably she will peck you, but it doesn't hurt. Then she will make a noise like a cat on steroids purring, and you know that you have a broody hen. Leave her for another day to become totally secure.

If you are really skilful you will have been saving the eggs from your best laying hens for the previous ten days, and certainly with experience you will try to do this; otherwise collect the good eggs from these last couple of days, add any (even from the fridge) that you know to be less than two weeks old, and you have a clutch of eggs to set. For some reason eggs are always set in uneven numbers for best results. Fertility in eggs goes off steadily after they are laid, and in the spring it does pay to date all the good eggs. Ideal hatching eggs are taken from birds that have served you well. The eggs should be a good shape, large, and the hen should really be in her second laying year or more. Compromise on this and the resulting stock will be the poorer.

Eggs are so beautiful.

The broody needs a broody coop to house her; this is essentially another nestbox where she can sit quietly on her eggs. You will need to lift her off the nest once a day and shut her away from her eggs for ten minutes while she eats, drinks and produces the most enormous turd. Make sure she does this, or the nest will end up a real mess. She can then go back for another twenty-four hour stint.

Other considerations will further affect your design of broody coop:

- Moisture. To get a good balance of humidity within the egg it pays to lift the broody hen off fairly early in the day while there is still some moisture in the grass so that this will be trans-mitted back to the nest. The box should therefore preferably be of a waterproof outside design rather than indoors. You are aiming for the conditions as near as possible to those of a dry hedge bottom (without foxes).
- No light is necessary but good ventila-tion is required.
- She will not sit 'tight' for long before needing to turn the eggs (to stop the chicks sticking to the inside of the shells) and make herself comfortable, so it must be big enough for her to do this.

If the pen does not have a run, that is fine (until the chicks hatch) but attach a soft string to her leg while she is off the nest both to keep her off and ensure she does not get distracted from getting a crop full of food and an empty digestive tract. Never rely on the intelligence of a hen! Try to have a run constructed in time for the chicks (twenty-one days, or twenty for bantams).

After the requisite number of days the chicks will hatch. It is extremely tempting to help slow hatching chicks out of the shell, but really it is better not to; the ones that don't want to come out probably should not. They have food enough from absorbing the egg sack to last at least twenty-four hours without further food; after that they must have food and water constantly. We buy commercial chick crumbs: I know what we have said about additives, but I have not researched the world over for additive-free chick crumbs, we just buy a couple of kilos to see them on their way and after a month or so they eat the same as everything else. On the small scale, and with traditional breeds, growers' rations (even if you can find additive-free ones) are probably not worth the bother.

Sometimes a good laying bird stops laying to go broody. She will probably not sit well enough to hatch anything, and you may not want to hatch anything. She must then be 'broken', which means keeping her uncomfortable enough to forget that she was going broody. Traditionally a pen was constructed with a slatted bottom to achieve this, but we generally put them in with a pen of fattener rabbits, which, by running around, prevent her settling down for too long. The process usually lasts about three days.

THE HARVEST

You don't need me to tell you how to collect eggs, except perhaps to say try not to disturb birds on the nestbox, and control your excitement until they come off. They shout about it with such vigour that you always know when they have laid.

If we assume that you will periodically hatch replacement birds there will also be a meat crop. Your ambition must be to keep a majority of your laying hens under three years of age, and to a significant degree your breeding programme is designed to provide replacements for the older hens. This gives old hens as a source of meat, and because you cannot choose the gender of eggs, young cockerels to eat as well. Old hens may not be very fat but they do have a very good flavour indeed, if only for soup.

Killing

Poultry of this size is generally killed by stretching the neck. If you are right-handed, hold the bird by its legs in your left hand (you may wish to gather up the wing tips too). Take the head in your right (comb in palm) and extend it as far as it naturally goes. Then bend it back and pull quickly downwards until the neck gives. The bird is now dead, but it is a good idea to check that the head is well separated from the bones of the neck; this gives an area for the blood to drain into. Others simply take their birds to the butcher. Never undertake killing things if you run the risk of messing it up: it's horrible.

Brace yourself for the fact that, however you kill it, a chicken will flap for a minute or so after it is dead. If the head is sepa-rate from the neck it is dead; this is just a nervous reflex, but it can be quite disturbing until you are used to it.

Plucking

Next is plucking. Keep the bird upside down, hanging by its legs from a string or similar. Pull the large feathers out of the wings first, then move on to the smaller ones. Be as gentle as you can, especially over the breast, as tearing the skin does spoil the appearance of the bird. The secret is not to try and pull too many feathers out with each plucking action.

Ribs and legs from an old bird.

If time is at a premium try skipping the whole of this stage (and the guts bit below). Slit the skin on the breast and cut the breast meat off. With a sharp knife running over the ribs this comes quite easy with practice. Then cut off the legs, and cut off and skin the leg joints. Use the rest as fertilizer. This process should save quite a lot of time and doesn't waste a significant amount.

Gutting

If you have plucked you will then need to gut the birds. Cut off the head and feet (at the joint where feathers meet scales). Make an incision from the top of the ribcage along the neck. Peel back and take out the crop (full of half digested food), then put your finger back in and loosen the remaining guts at this end. Then make another cut from the bottom of the ribcage towards the vent. Divert just before reaching the vent and go right around it and back to your cut. Beware the two sharp bones on either side of the vent; if you cut yourself with these the cut is always slow to heal, so be careful.

You now have access to the internal cavity. Pull out the intestines and every-thing else mostly through the back, but the top can be used for part. Cut off the neck and the carcass is ready to truss. Nothing clever in trussing: just make it look right and then tie the legs together to hold it in place. One point to note is to use proper butcher's string; other string may melt or taint the meat on cooking.

The guts can be sorted through for heart, kidneys and liver, all of which can be used in cooking even if only for stock. The neck, too, makes good stock. However, beware the small sack of fluid on the livers: this is the gall bladder. Ensure it is intact, and then remove it by grasping the base between thumb and forefinger and pulling it away. If the fluid is spilt, the liver will taste horrible, and you will have to throw it away.

Allow the carcass to set before use.

DUCKS

All breeds of domestic duck with the exception of the Muscovy are descended from the wild mallard. Selective breeding over the centuries has brought their size from a nice snack to a meal for the family. The Muscovy – also known as the Barbary duck – is a wild species of the American tropics; together with the turkey, these are the only farmed birds that originated in the New World.

Ducks fall into two main groups: layers and table ducks, and in both categories quite spectacular results are achieved. Where hens lay 300 eggs in a year, many ducks will lay 330. Table ducks are on the table at twelve weeks old, well ahead of most hens. For these levels of performance you will need a high protein ration. It may now be possible to find additive-free ones and this may help, but sensible duck keeping should avoid these high performance birds, and any feed will need to be supplemented by some grain.

First let us look at laying ducks: of their 330 eggs each they will lay 20 per cent where you will never find them (even under water), 50 per cent in so much mud that you cannot face eating them (rightly), and the remaining 30 per cent may be left for you.

Table ducks need to be sorted through a bit. The standard Aylesbury type is very quick growing and very nice to eat, but is still not a patch on wild duck. Some of the other improved wild duck varieties are less 'improved' than others, retaining better flavours, and I favour the Rouen amongst these. The Muscovy is also worth a try.

The first problem with ducks is that they are water birds, and most need some water if only to mate in. As a general rule, unless you have some water I don't think they should be kept, and if it is not much, you need to be able to clean it out regularly as ducks foul their water constantly. Ducks being wet when they come from the water make mud; the mud spoils the grass, and to that mixture of mud and grass they add droppings in copious quantities. Somehow they will add mud to their food as well.

The secret is to avoid overstocking and a pair or two may still be an attractive proposition.

Stock may be acquired either as adults or as ducklings, but the best policy is probably to set eggs under a broody hen. She will get everything right except for one thing: not being a duck, she will fail to transfer waterproofing oils to the ducklings, so they must be kept off water until they get their adult feathers. Feed ducklings with chick crumbs like chicks. Incubation takes twenty-eight days.

One of the attractions of ducks is that you can feed them all your table scraps. They are omnivores and, unlike pigs, there are no legal restrictions on their diets. If you have a family member who consistently leaves their food, then ducks may

Some Aylesbury-type ducklings at about four weeks old foraging well.

be just the perfect recycling machine. They will also need to be fed some grain and a higher protein ration.

In practice most ducks destroy grass rather than eat it. Muscovys are an exception and if you want a small area grazed try them. Otherwise try geese.

Since it is almost inevitable that in a small area all will be turned to mud by ducks, either range them and rotate them over a large area, or accept the mud. I must admit that this is what I like least about ducks, and managing to avoid mud causes great problems for us.

Table ducks will lay a clutch of eggs in the spring, which can either be eaten or set under a broody hen or a mixture of both. Some ducks can make quite good mothers (but a broody is better). If you keep taking the eggs away they will lay more of them than they otherwise would.

Harvest as for hens.

GEESE

If you were thinking of table ducks, then perhaps geese would be better. The carcass is obviously bigger, although not much so for some breeds, but geese are much more suited to living without water than ducks. They can get a very large proportion of their own food from grazing, and some grain as supplementary feed is all they generally need. They do share with ducks an ability to make grassland messy quite quickly, but by comparison with ducks, they are rank amateurs in the muck stakes.

Probably the commonest geese are the type known as Embden Toulouse. Strictly these are two different varieties crossed for hybrid vigour, but very often the crosses are bred together again and again, and they have become rather a type. Others are Roman (smaller and quieter), and Chinese (much noisier). If you need guard dogs, geese may be better; if not, the noise can be annoying.

On the garden scale foie gras production would be possible, but it is time-consuming and contentious. We grow geese occasionally but only for eating the carcass.

Once again the broody hen is a good source of goslings, though you will have to be patient, as the hatching period is longer, at about twenty-eight days. There is one important detail to know with geese (and with ducks, too, though to a lesser extent) relating to humidity: being waterfowl, they have adapted to being incubated by mothers who return to the nest with wet feathers after feeding. Rather than dunk your hen in the pond daily, just splash the eggs with water flicked from your hand while the hen is feeding; literally only a few drops. Failure to do this results in dry membranes, making hatching difficult. After hatching, flick water over the goslings in the same way for a few days until they go out on grass, or you will get quite high mortality rates.

From after the first two days make sure the goslings can get to fresh grass, and in a few weeks they will be eating plenty of it; until then chick crumbs will suffice.

Geese hatched in the spring are normally eaten any time from Michaelmas to Christmas, though can be run on a little longer if required.

Killing

A different killing technique is required for big birds. Some take a post a little less than a metre long and cut a notch in it sufficient to accommodate the bird's neck. They then hold the bird by its legs in the usual way, lay its neck on the ground, lay the post over its neck and hold with the feet. Then pull.

I am not ashamed to admit that I get the butcher to kill them; if you can find one that will still do it, it's a lot easier.

PIGEONS

Pigeons should mainly be acknowledged in a book such as this under the heading 'Pests'. We have to cover many of our vegetables, especially brassicas and peas, to keep them from destroying our crops. Fortunately we also manage to catch a few of them and they taste very good indeed. Gardening is the next stage up from hunting, and if the valuable vegetables are covered already, there is merit in considering pigeons as a crop. As for the effect on your neighbours' vegetable patch, I leave you to fight your own battles!

Pigeons are kept in a variety of lofts, but any system which does not let them outside seems to me to be no better than any other factory farming. The system should therefore let them range. However, a secure loft has to be built as a starting point because pigeons have to be brought in as adults or juveniles but not as chicks, and their homing instincts are known to all. They can be let out when they have bred their own young, as from then on that is where they will home to.

Pigeons feed their young by regurgitating food to them, which comes out as a milky substance. This is a very high protein diet and the squabs grow fast. Usually they lay two eggs each time and the squabs should be eaten before they get their adult feathers at six weeks old or less. Well managed, each pair of pigeons can produce up to four clutches – eight squabs – per year. Pluck and prepare as for other poultry.

The nestboxes required are the classic dovecotes of old. Many dovecotes had stacks of boxes running to hundreds, with complicated systems of ladders for access. Perhaps we should be looking to house up to three or maybe four pairs; otherwise we could easily have too many squabs.

The feed for pigeons is grain, but generally enhanced with some peas. For once your local feed merchant will probably supply a good mixture which is not processed unduly. It will be the same mixture as the racing pigeon people use.

GUINEA FOWL AND QUAIL

Good though they taste, both guinea fowl and quail are wild birds only relatively recently domesticated. For good results they should be kept with considerable range; when closely confined their health risks increase. Commercial feeds of course address this with additives.

We are currently experimenting with quail and I shall write further about them in the future if we have any success.

For those with more space, treat guinea fowl as hens but accept that they will roost in trees if let out. They also make a terrible noise, which on summer mornings could make you less than popular with your neighbours.

TURKEYS

Again, turkeys should have space, which makes them less ideal for small gardens. If you do have a patch of ground try one of the old breeds and rotate them regularly on to fresh pasture. Do not overstock; the disease caused by overstocking nearly wiped out the early turkey industry.

Beware too the fox. These birds are not able to protect themselves even by perching at a decent height and we have had to concede that we cannot grow them; this is a shame, because old breed turkey is very special on the table.

CHAPTER 12

Pigs

For generations the sty at the bottom of the garden was a reality for very many people, and it is still viable today.

I like pigs. After a stressful day of awkward clients and public transport disruption it is good to know that something will listen to you and make all the right noises (especially if receiving a scratch on the back at the time). The sight of a large sow collapsing in ecstasy from this treatment restores your faith in your own nature.

I also love good pork, and it bears no relationship whatsoever to the stuff you buy in the supermarkets. Our experience shows that several factors affect the flavour of pork:

- The feeding regime.
- The variety of pig: this is a very significant item, often ignored in the quest for fast-growing, cheap meat. Remember the huge premium paid for the meat of wild boar, and there is a whole spectrum of flavours between that and modern hybrid pig.
- The speed of growth; on our scale we can allow a little longer to reach killing weight – and the bland stuff does grow very fast indeed.
- The age and size of the pig when killed.

Commercial pig feeds will often include growth promoters and all the other wonders of the modern feed industry.

Feeding a pig at home enables us to avoid, or at least reduce, these.

With the ability to produce more than twenty young per sow per annum, the risk is that you will have more meat from one sow than most families can eat. We therefore have two possible strategies:

- Buy in weaners (usually eight-week-old youngsters) once or twice a year. Fatten them and put them in the freezer at a size and weight to suit you (more on this later).
- Keep one sow and find a market for the excess weaners. This is much the most pleasurable system, but has two main problems: the housing requirement is much greater, and the sows need access to a boar, which can be difficult. Since we enjoy breeding pigs a later book will inevitably deal with breeding, but it is not within the practical scope of most gardeners and is not included here.

Before getting into pigs, get prepared. A good breeder will normally let you look at their stock, and you can go back to collect the chosen ones when they are about eight weeks old. This gives you time to prepare, as you will need accommodation ready for them together with troughs, feed and straw. You will also need to review your domestic arrangements for managing

Just under eight weeks old. Two Oxford Sandy and Black weaners.

wellington boots and overalls, because pigs will cause you to use these items more than any of the stock we have talked about so far.

Get the publication from DEFRA A Guide to New Owners, Pigs. Although it avoids several important issues concerning killing, it does give a lot of good guidance. Furthermore you are now into cloven-hoofed livestock and will need to register your 'holding' with the Rural Payments Agency.

Think also about transport issues. If the pigs can be delivered to you, that is all well and good – but later on how will you get them to the abattoir? Think before you rush into it. Incidentally horseboxes (your own or borrowed) are often not a very good idea for pigs. They work well enough, but the smell of pigs can cause a normally

good-natured horse to refuse to be boxed ever again. Whatever you use will need to be cleaned very carefully after use, by law.

HOUSING

These days it is not unusual to see large herds of pigs living outside, and if you have the space this is a pleasant way to keep pigs; also the equipment, including housing, is widely available. However, on the garden scale it is unlikely that you will be able to allow them this much freedom, and the old-fashioned sty remains an excellent building for pigs. This book assumes that the small-scale keeper will bed his pigs on straw, in that strawy manure for the muck heap is an important

Modest but adequate pig accommodation.

by-product of pig keeping. Mud is not attractive stuff, and a pig outside must have enough space to ensure access to reasonably clean ground on a frequent basis otherwise we are up against the true 'pig in s**t', which is not a happy animal nor pleasant to live alongside.

Pig accommodation should be sited away from the immediate vicinity of the house; pigs do attract flies and a certain amount of vermin, although with care this can be avoided as it is mainly the spilt food that brings them in. The issue of smell, although often overstated, also encourages the pig-keeping enterprise to be sited at the bottom of the garden. In fact the only time we were ever worried by the smell of pigs was when we bought in some weaners from a commercial farmer, and they smelled from day one. Our own rarely offend the most

sensitive of noses, and my theory is that different breeds smell different; but I have yet to hear that opinion voiced by anyone else. Certainly they must be mucked out daily to keep smells down, but done daily it is not too much of a chore. Boars will also smell more than sows.

If you have buildings they can be adapted to house pigs, though certain rules should be observed. First, they must be able to sleep away from draughts, preferably on a wooden or insulated floor. Second, there must be adequate ventilation; this apparent contradiction is at the heart of all livestock accommodation, but hot air having risen, it must be allowed out, and the cooler air coming in to replace it must not flow over the animals. Allow 15sq m (161sq ft) for a sow; about 6sq m (64.5sq ft) would be acceptable for a pair of weaners.

Pigs are strong, and you will get into all sorts of trouble if you don't build accordingly. Make the pen walls and gates strong enough to keep them in when they use the weakest point on which to scratch themselves (a sow may approach a third of a ton in weight).

Lastly, avoid extremes of temperature. The cold is easy and can be accommodated by extra straw, but hot days require a well insulated roof. Do beware of corrugated iron roofs when the pig kept outside cannot get away from the heat. Beware, too, of forcing them to lie in the sun when they would prefer the shade, because the pink-skinned breeds in particular are prone to sunburn; I often worry about these big outside herds and whether some of them really offer enough shade.

The outside sty is our preference. The pigs can lean over the gate and watch what is going on, food can be chucked at them whenever you have it in your hands, and generally pigs seem contented that way. The basic rules are the same as outlined above. A sty for a pair of weaners being reared to pork weight (the smallest of the normal killing weights, except for sucking pig and they are killed before weaning) need be no more than a house of about 2sq m (20sq ft) with a run perhaps one and a half or two times the size of the building. We prefer to make our sties a little bigger, but then we rear more than two at a time and sometimes to a greater weight. Beware, however, because if the house is too much bigger the piglets are far more likely to foul part of the house, rather than going outside to do it.

Start with a good concrete base. Make sure that it slopes away from the place where the pigs will sleep as a wet bed will be a disaster. The house needs to be about 2m (6 to 7ft) tall at the front with a doorway in it. The doorway should be full height so that you can get in when you need to, and is generally fitted with half a door at the top. The top remains closed to reduce drafts and the pigs have free access through the lower half to what is their sleeping area. Some people cover the floor of the sleeping area with boards or insulate under the concrete base to keep them warm, but we just use plenty of straw. Pigs can be destructive and simple structures are usually more durable. The roof should slope to the rear to keep the water out of the run.

A run is then built in front, which must contribute to keeping the draughts down with fairly solid walls and a gate. Again, concrete is best for the floor.

Materials are a matter of choice but need to be strong. Concrete blocks and bricks are good, but it is perfectly possible to build from wood assuming planks of at least 3cm (1in) thick and stout posts (on the outside of the boards for strength). The most destructive technique the pig has, especially if you let them get a bit too big, is simply to lean, usually when scratching.

BUYING AND YOUR CHOICE OF BREED

One of the difficulties of electing to buy in weaners for fattening is that you may have little practical choice over varieties. You will get all sorts of flavour advantages anyway from your feeding regimes, so it is still worth doing, but it has to be said that once you have found one of the really fine flavour breeds you will wish to stick with it. Bear in mind that the Vietnamese Pot-Bellied pig so beloved of the pet owners of California is not a serious contender: they are slow-growing, have poor flavour and above all are fatty. Leave well alone.

Breed	Taste	Comments
Berkshire	Good	Nice pigs
Gloucester Old Spot	Good	Somewhat over-rated, in my opinion, because it looks nice and is nicknamed the 'orchard pig' (but most pigs eat apples)
Hybrid pigs	Commercial	Usually Large White based
Landrace	Ordinary but very lean	Not as hardy as some
Large White	Ordinary commercial	Will never be as interesting as a minority breed
Large Black	A lot better than some	Reputation for quiet temperament
Middle White	Commercial	Some love them
Oxford Sandy and Black	Wonderful	Without doubt my personal favourite
Saddleback	Not bad at all	There used to be Essex and Wessex Saddlebacks and the distinction had been lost, however the separate lines are appearing again
Tamworth	Very good	Some doubts over temperament
Welsh	Fairly commercial	A smaller pig

World-wide there are dozens of varieties, all of which have their fans. The best possible recommendation comes from a good meal. You might just wish to consider wild boar and they are included in the last chapter for the more adventurous. For most of us, however, unless you have sufficient space over which to range them, don't even think of it.

If you are going to have a surplus that needs to be sold you will have to consider colour prejudice. Quite genuinely most commercial pork buyers want white-skinned pigs and there is, as far as I know, as little justification for that, as for other colour prejudices. Colour tolerance may be increasing now even commercially, and certainly discriminating eaters look to flavour before colour.

Whatever you intend to do, even if you want to keep a sow, the best place to start is with two weaners: two, simply because they do better, and need less attention than one. If you are to keep a sow, get two females otherwise it doesn't matter too much, but the same sex is easier than one of each. For pigs, like modern children, sex becomes an issue far too soon.

FEEDING

Every school child knows that pigs will eat almost anything and are efficient converters of waste food to meat. What unfortunately gets in the way of making the best of this is the law. I will not claim

Our much loved Oxford Sandy and Black sow 'The Duchess'.

for a moment that there is anything wrong with the law, which is designed to prevent the transmission of some quite horrible diseases, just that it makes life difficult.

The rules are that you may not have on your premises for the purpose of feeding them to livestock any feed containing meat, bones, blood, offal, or even eggs, nor anything that has been in contact with them, unless it is processed by feed manufacturers or otherwise processed under license. Practically speaking, the hoops to jump through to obtain a license are not worth even looking at for the small producer.

Since the latest foot and mouth epidemic the restrictions on bringing food on to the premises have been tightened still further, but it still leaves all the food that we can grow for them.

On the scale that we are considering here, and let's not forget that we still have to get to work in the morning, a majority of the pigs' usual ration will come out of a bag. At the very least we need some easy food for the tough days even if we are aiming to be in control of the ration most of the time. As with other stock there is no point in going to the pet shop: for serious animal food the local feed mills will have to be researched. Organic feeds are beginning now to be available, and if available locally these would be ideal; but very

often, especially if they have to be carried any distance, the cost is prohibitive.

Specialist pig feeds, especially for growers, contain most of the additives which I, for one, would rather avoid. Sow feed, by contrast, tends to contain less of these things, and as a result we feed what is known as 'sow breeder meal' to our growers. A little extra milk in the feed can help in the first two weeks to get the protein levels even higher, but that should be all that is required. Do not leave stale milk in the troughs; it will do much harm in the early weeks.

Amounts of food are the subject of enormous amounts of research. Pig feed is usually expressed in terms of barley meal equivalent, and books are full of tables giving amounts to feed to pigs, assuming that every time you chuck a bucket of slug-ridden potatoes to them you will convert it to barley meal equivalent and reduce the next meal accordingly. Add to this the complication that modern pigs convert food to weight at a ratio of around 3:1 and old breeds may be as 'bad' as 5:1, and this all becomes too much trouble.

Judgement is very useful. Think about the amount of scraps and garden produce they are getting when measuring out their feed. As a rough guide, assuming reasonable amounts of vegetable matter to eat as well, and that there is always straw to

FOOD FROM THE GARDEN FOR PIGS

Pigs are such catholic eaters that no list can be complete, but grow for bulk when you have pigs. Consider the following as almost essential:

- Vegetable plants when finished
- Fodder beet
- Jerusalem artichoke tubers
- Potatoes, parsnips and leeks (cooked is much more nourishing than raw, but if you cook it in your domestic kitchen, it will be illegal to feed this as it will be catering waste)
- Swede and turnip
- Windfall apples

chew on, feed as much as they will eat in 20 minutes twice a day. That should be self balancing, but adjust according to condition: more if they look thin and less if they look fat. Look at other peoples' pigs if you are in doubt, because you will learn more from looking and talking than any book can tell you.

To get you going (assuming you have bought in weaners at eight weeks old), allow them a kilo each split into two feeds per day, and you will not be far wrong. As they get bigger they will need more, up to nearly twice as much by the time they are ready for killing, when they will weigh 50kg (110lb) or more.

HEALTH

In many years of keeping pigs we have had only a few reasons to call the vet, and all of them for breeding matters. There are,

however, a few things that you should have to hand. The first essential is purple spray, available from agricultural sundriesmen and useful for all minor cuts and abrasions, also any minor inflammations. Then once or twice we have had an attack of mange on some bought-in stock: it happens, and the sundriesmen should be able to supply a preparation for that, too. Mange is a small parasite and lives under the skin; if you are observant you should see it start both with small red marks on the skin and because the animals start to scratch themselves too much.

As a beginner accept that there are times when the vet will have to be called and paid for. They will show you how to administer injections and other remedies until you feel confident.

Always put new stock in clean housing. Use Jeyes fluid or similar disinfectants to get houses really clean.

That should cover it unless you are very unlucky. If in doubt with pigs you should call a vet because some diseases are notifiable (in other words you must tell the ministry, and the vet will know if this is necessary).

HARVESTING

Traditionally pigs are kept to about 55kg (120lb) liveweight for pork and up to as much as 100kg (220lb) for bacon. Other weights are also used, but for our purposes the supply of food will also influence when you slaughter. There is, in my experience, nothing wrong with pork from a larger carcass than normal, except that the joints are larger. What hardship! The one caution here is that heavier pigs may be more prone to fat depending on breed and how you feed them; you will learn by experience.

Be sure you know how the pigs will be killed even before you start to keep them, otherwise you have a problem. For most people a local slaughterhouse is the best option; I don't think home killing is currently an option (*see* Chapter 9). Ring around and see who will take your pigs; some slaughterhouses will not take pigs from small producers.

For the beginner it is very difficult to judge how big your pigs really are. Obviously a set of scales would be very useful, but pig scales are not the sort of thing we all have in our sheds (well, we did, but they took up too much space). Use a thing called a weighband, which is no more than a dressmakers' tape measure calibrated in pig weights. It is not accurate, but it is certainly good enough for general purposes.

We have sent pigs both to commercial slaughterhouses and had them killed at home. When we were still able to kill them at home we felt part of a very traditional process. In societies all around the world killing the pig is an excuse for great celebration. Until we can do it again this chapter remains a bit shorter than it perhaps should be.

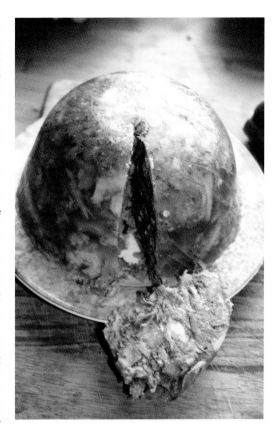

Make sure you get the head and trotters back from your butcher. They make lovely brawn.

CHAPTER 13

Goats

Of all the livestock that we have kept, dairy goats give the least pleasure. They are nevertheless worthy of serious attention. They are more compact than a cow, their milk is nutritious, of a good flavour (if you get it right), and usable by people allergic to or intolerant of cow's milk. In addition, to milk them you must breed from them and the resulting kids produce meat like lamb with less fat (although it is slower growing). Goats also provide skins, hair (the Angora goat produces mohair and the Kashmir produces cashmere) and, in theory at least, they can be used as draught animals. None of these last magnificent attributes is likely to be of practical use unless you have a lot of time and energy, and they will not be pursued further here.

Why then, do I not like them and leave them to the end of the book? The main reasons are as follows:

■ The noise. A goat trying to attract your attention does not bleat (the official term): it blithers. It goes on blithering until you have second-guessed its every need and fully satisfied it. By then it wants something else.
■ Milking animals are beyond the limits of what we can mix with an ordinary working life. The milking routine of twice a day is bad enough, but they also need to be fed and inspected several times a day.

■ They will escape – there are no 'ifs', it is just a question of 'when'. They will then seriously damage all your growing crops, prize roses and laundry.
■ The need for a billy goat. Even if you are lucky enough to be able to use somebody else's billy, the smell that will attach to your nanny for the next week or so is a serious consideration, and it will attach itself to you. You cannot go to the office smelling like that and expect to keep your job.

There is a possibility now gaining currency to keep goats purely for meat. In the same way that, in mainstream agriculture, suckler cattle are becoming an ever more popular beef production technique, on the garden scale it is possible to keep suckler goats for kids. Where sheep are a bit limiting as the mainstay of their diet is grass, the catholicism of a goat's diet is legendary (and true), which enables them to be kept in small spaces with food brought to them. A particular trend has grown up for the Boer goat, which is very expensive and considered most suitable for this technique; however, some of the established breeds will do perfectly well.

On this basis it is possible to operate at lower levels of performance than for dairy goats, and with that comes a reduction in stress for the animals and an easier (perhaps slightly quieter) regime for the goat keeper.

Goats are large animals and they eat a lot. When you start thinking about goats, consider how much food you gather for perhaps twenty rabbits, and assuming you can double it you may be able to graduate to them; otherwise you will be relying a lot on expensive, bought-in food.

HOUSING

Two types of accommodation can be used: either a pen can be partitioned off in an existing building, or a house and yard similar to a pigsty can be built for the job. The main requirements of both are that there should be a raised, draught-free platform on which to sleep, and enough space: 4sq m (4.8sq yd) should be enough. In a shed several can be housed together, which gives them company and is one less reason for blithering.

The structure need be less strong than for pigs, but must still be fairly robust as goats do like to put their front feet on things to extend their reach and area of vision – so be warned.

A good goat house which, with a small run, will hold several goats.

BUYING

Assuming that you will only be looking for meat and not for milk, buy a big goat. If you are looking for a milking goat despite my advice, go for a Toggenburg, especially if you are a beginner. They are the quietest (least noisy) of them all. The best milkers are generally the British Saanens and the British Alpines, although many skilled breeders get excellent performances out of many breeds.

For meat the breed is unimportant, but the larger ones are probably going to be Anglo-Nubian or one of the specialist meat goats such as the Boer or the Spanish – but pure-bred stock of these is generally expensive.

Resist the temptation to buy the small breeds on the grounds that they can't be as much trouble. Pygmy and other small goats possess all the worst qualities of their larger brethren, and when you come to kill them (in desperation or otherwise) the joints are at best disappointing.

FEEDING

Having got this far, if you are going ahead, you have more time than I now do, but we must consider how to keep them simply and with a minimum of time and effort. The standard way of keeping a goat is to tether it in a field or patch of scrub. If you do this you must be there to untangle it when the tether gets snarled up and to bring it in when the weather gets too unkind. It is nevertheless a good way of feeding goats the fresh food that they thrive on.

Otherwise the goats can be kept in their pens and the food brought to them. You will need either to visit them four times a day or to have two large mangers; one constantly full of hay (keep the bars close together to minimize waste) and the other filled with green material before you go to work every day and again when you get home. The list of suitable green feed is exactly as for rabbits.

In either case they will also need hard feed at least twice a day; the quantity is the amount that they clear up in 15 minutes. This regime is even then only a compromise as the goat is a ruminant and needs to eat little and often to get the best from its food. One test showed that you needed twice as much feed per litre of milk if the goat was fed once a day as if she were fed five times a day; but which of us can commit to feeding that often?

With goats, as with rabbits, the hard feed needs to be as close as possible to 18 per cent protein, and again this can be achieved in a variety of ways, but I would suggest that local feed merchants be scoured to find additive-free feeds of as high a protein content as possible. If the only protein levels available are under 17 per cent you will have to feed something as a supplement. Lucerne would do fine in the summer, but you will need either lucerne or clover hay in the winter, or maybe pea straw if you can get it, to replace part of the hay ration.

BREEDING

You will get neither meat nor milk, normally, without taking the nanny to the billy. Having said that, I have known 'maiden milkers' give a litre a day – but you cannot rely on them.

Find a billy goat as big as possible for meat and as well bred as possible if you really intend to keep any offspring to increase your milk supply. Wait until the

A young female British Alpine goat.

goat is in season; this first occurs every summer sometimes in August, always by September and then for a few months on a twenty-one day cycle. Line out the car carefully and take the nanny to the billy. The mating process is unexceptional and little assistance is normally required. Do, however, ensure that the billy owner is satisfied that the job has been done, and agree between you that if your nanny comes back into season twenty-one days later, you can return. Her season is usually apparent from behaviour changes, but also from a slight sticky discharge from a somewhat enlarged vulva.

Wait three months, three weeks and three days. Birth will not occur dead on time but close to the appointed time usually on a misty night; goats seem to like the moisture and perhaps your absence. If you do see things going wrong, call the vet or someone with experience. Birthing large animals is best learnt first hand and not from books – but be reassured, goats usually manage well on their own.

You must make sure that new-born kids find the mother's teats within the first few hours, and they may need help for this (did I mention that goats are not terribly intelligent?). Thereafter things can take care of themselves. If you want to milk the goat, start as soon as the colostrum has given way to 'normal' milk, on about day three (colostrum is the milk that all animals produce just after giving birth; it

A pen of young billy goats whose future is as meat.

contains not only milk for nourishment, but also a raft of other substances to stimulate the immune and digestive systems of the young). Don't drink the goat's milk for the first few days as it will contain enough colostrum still to upset your stomach, but the goat's milk production will be greater if she is milked out by you twice a day as well as by the kids in between. Otherwise she will reduce her output to match their needs only (which is fine for meat-only production).

After a couple of weeks the young kids will start to eat a little hay and some hard feed. Assuming regular greenstuff is available and ad lib hay, then feed only the amount that they eat up in 20 minutes. Do not be over-generous with concentrates as it can turn to fat.

HARVESTING

It is best to ask an experienced goatkeeper how to milk. The basic rules are that they are not milked like cows where you use a downward stripping motion. Instead, close off the top of the teat with thumb and first finger and then close your other fingers over the teat to squeeze out the milk. Repeat until no more comes out. Then gently massage the whole udder and repeat the process – it takes half an hour twice a day. This massage, known as stripping out, is very important; otherwise yields drop off rapidly.

Killing is covered generally in Chapter 9. The killing time will be dictated as much by the falling availability of food in the late autumn as by the weight of the animals.

CHAPTER 14

Other Large Animals

With the exception of pigs and goats, large animals do not easily adapt to being kept in small areas mainly because grass is the major part of their diet. If you have some grass then it might be fun to try some of these.

SHEEP

Sheep are an almost sensible option for people with space. They can be left to their own devices for at least some of the time, and the fencing can be relatively cheap (including electric fencing which is not so good for most other stock).

I have the greatest respect for some of the so-called 'primitive' sheep, but they should be avoided unless you are experienced. We used to keep Soay sheep, but the category encompasses Hebridean, Ronaldsay and many other small varieties. Soays are one of the oldest unimproved wild sheep varieties (actually in the last half century I think they have improved somewhat from selective breeding) and wild sheep have survived as long as they have by being intelligent, resourceful and thrifty. Hidden in that list is a slight problem. When being resourceful they

have developed an ability to look after themselves, which can surprise. Our greatest mistake was to borrow some grazing from friends several miles away on which to put these sheep. The 'phone call duly came on a cold New Year's morning 'They're out!'. We and half the local population spent a futile day chasing these sheep over hectares of arable fields without any barriers, only to find that they went back in, all by themselves (through the hole they had made) as soon as it got dark. On another occasion, one jumped clean over a fence just to join some passing horses.

We learned to keep them close to home and to give them enough attention and food to keep them a little tame.

The safer option is almost certainly to have fewer, larger, more modern sheep. These generally do not have the energy for such antics and are easier to manage. You get more meat per sheep, but the flavour is nothing like so good as that of my primitive friends.

It is not good enough to leave sheep entirely to their own devices and to rely on grass alone; if you do they will certainly become wild, whereas given a little food they will grow much better. If kept over

Spring lamb is a joy to observe as well as to eat.

winter, watch the mud (ideally bring them indoors) and feed them plenty of hay. Feeding hay is not always easy, and some sheep have to learn to eat it (yes really!); it must therefore be offered in good time as a supplement before they need it.

Remember with sheep as with all outdoor stock to rotate the land. Divide it into at least two sections and allow one part to rest while the other is being grazed; if you do not, the ground will become stale, the sheep will not eat the grass and, more importantly, parasites will build up. Worm them a few days before putting them on fresh ground. Forget about milk sheep; you are a farmer by this stage and out of our league.

The two bugbears of sheep keeping are dipping and shearing. Sheep dipping has not been required for several years now, but if DEFRA says you must use it, there is no option. If that happens, get in touch with a local sheep farmer and persuade them to dip your sheep with theirs otherwise it simply is not practical.

Shearing is also probably best done when your local farmer has his sheep done. A few varieties (Soay is one) shed their wool and do not need to be shorn. Lambs are killed before they need to be shorn.

Start by buying a few lambs in spring and rearing them for meat. Buy from late-born flocks so that you have grass to feed them on (January born is no use at all) at about fourteen weeks old and keep them while the grass is good. Killing can be at any time, but I think flavour improves with a little age, and would be quite happy taking them on until the grass runs out in September. Try not to overfeed with concentrates as they will get fat. When the grass is good you are only doing it to keep them tame; after that give them no more than they can clear up in 10 minutes.

Sheep really are prone to quite a lot of very unpleasant parasites; keep an eye on their rear ends, clip off anything that looks unpleasant on the wool, and if maggots appear, get them off and apply purple spray.

CATTLE

This section is included for the sake of completeness, but for a gardener, cattle are just not realistic. Whilst they can use up your surplus grass, a milking animal of this size is really beyond the scope of gardens. For those with an adjacent paddock a few bullocks (steers) for meat would be possible. These are neutered males; if you intend to keep bulls – males that have not been neutered – then you will have to inform the bureaucrats and they might not allow you to do so. This is a shame because bulls grow faster and more efficiently than bullocks.

Having discounted cows as not practical and discouraged goat keeping, if you have concerns about commercially produced milk the question of home-produced milk has still not been resolved; but if for any reason you really want to produce your own milk, then your commitment to your garden farm will need to be greater than this book envisages. Remember we are trying to keep a steady job as well as doing all this, so for me the solution is the milkman.

If you are still not discouraged, try Dexter cattle. A least, being small, they will cut down the milk surpluses a little; a full sized cow produces around 15ltr (3gal) of milk a day at peak times (though remember that for some weeks you will get none at all). But even with a smaller cow, milking is still a tedious chore.

One other thought for the paddock is a suckler cow. Here the cow kept apart from her calf but let in twice a day to feed it after you have taken some milk for the house; otherwise the calf will drink all of the milk.

CALVES

One other way of keeping cattle is to rear calves. I enjoy rearing calves, but am not sure that there is any risk reduction in my own food by doing so. When a calf is available for purchase it will have been removed from its mother so that her milk may be sold; we therefore have to feed it on milk substitute, a manufactured product full, possibly, of all the things that worry us most about modern food production. You may feel that, assuming you wish to have red veal rather than white (from the animals that live in crates and only

A nice Dexter cow.

ever drink this stuff) you can reduce risks. I guess you can, but milk substitutes are still a major part of their diet.

One ray of hope is that if you have ignored my advice on goats and cows you may have surplus milk, and this is indeed a good use of it. Calf feeding is easy: put two or three fingers in a calf's mouth and it will suck them, lower hand into a bucket of milk, calf will suck milk, remove fingers. Repeat until lesson fully learned. Alternatively use teats and bottles or pipes, but fingers are easiest.

Buy calves from a reputable herd where you know the calf will have drunk from its mother for the first few days and so will have received sufficient colostrum. As discussed above, colostrum contains all the necessary antibodies for survival. The vet is an expensive and ineffective substitute for this.

RATITES

Now here is an interesting proposition which the commercial sector cannot get right, and which with a little modification one should be able to develop on a small piece of grassland. The majority of the current work has been done on ostriches, but other birds in the group include emus, rheas (nandus) and others. A trio of ostriches requires less than 0.25ha (0.62acres).

The fundamental point of interest with these birds is that they produce red meat (and some very valuable feather and leather by-products), and they have very good food conversion ratios. Whereas for beef you will need upwards of 4.5kg (10lb) of feed for a single kilo (2.2lb) of meat, with this family you will produce the equivalent in meat from about 2kg (4.5lb) of food. This is extremely efficient. The reasons why not are interesting, but beyond the scope of this book.

The meat itself has a very low fat content, and of all the red meats is the lowest in cholesterol. The average weight of a bird killed at twelve to fifteen months old, the normal killing weight, is about 50kg (110lb), giving around 35–40kg (77–88lb) of meat per bird.

The real down side of ostriches is that for local authority registration purposes they are wild birds. They are big, they can be stroppy, and the terms of your licence may tie you to the premises all day. For me the idea of keeping them ends right here, but there are other members of the family that are much more practical, namely their South American relative, the rhea. These are smaller than ostriches (the carcass is typically 25kg/55lb) and do not require a wild animal licence; they can still be difficult birds but they are at least possible.

Allow space at the rate of twenty-five birds per hectare, though remember that young birds from about six months old will need their entitlement of space while being reared.

There is a problem with killing these birds in that very few abattoirs can handle them. There is no way that you will wring their necks, so you need to have found the solution to this one before you start.

Given good fencing and a rough shelter against the worst of the weather, this family will all do well. As with all stock it is advisable to divide their land preferably into two paddocks rotated to keep the ground sweet. They rotate quite well with sheep.

Visit twice a day to bribe them with grain and they will at least come close enough for you to establish that they are all right. Feed youngstock more often, and also feed more if the grass runs out (but try not to let the grass run out). Breeding hens may also be fed a little dog meat to advantage.

Buy no more than a breeding pair to start with. Eggs are laid in an open nest, and the male will attempt to incubate them. He can raise ten to fifteen chicks unassisted if left alone, but there will probably be more eggs than that laid, which will mean they don't get looked after very well. Until you know how many your hen lays each spring, take away the first ten for rheas and twenty for ostriches and see what you are left with for the male to incubate. The eggs you remove can either be put in an incubator or used for large omelettes.

If you do hatch in incubators remember that the chicks are quite vulnerable until three months old. Remember that although they need to be kept warm, they also need fresh air; therefore offer a heat lamp but ventilate well.

WILD BOAR

The wild boar is not a grassland creature, but one that needs space to be 'wild' and find a great part of its own food. Now quite popular as an alternative farm crop on the continent of Europe and in the States, there is absolutely no doubt that the flavour of wild boar is something quite special. They are, of course, not wild animals really: you need to feed them twice a day just like pigs, the only difference being that you can feed them a bit less. Nevertheless they are being farmed, and as intensity increases the special nature of the meat is being diluted – and in truth we have domestication all over again. Wouldn't pigs be easier?

Having said that, they are undoubtedly worth a try on a well fenced piece of rough land fit for nothing else, and you should get some fabulous meat, surprisingly lean and a culinary delight. But first of all be sure to register your boar with the local authority, as in their eyes these are wild animals.

APPENDIX

List of Varieties

The list below is based on the varieties we use, selected for flavour and ease of growing. It is worth also looking at your local market stalls, where the varieties traditionally successful in your area are likely to be available.

Asparagus
I still like Connovers Colossal, although there are lots of more modern varieties that the vendors speak highly of.

Beetroot
Bolthardy is the traditional favourite. Chioggia Barabietola is a good alternative – a paler colour.

Broad Beans
Aquadulce for autumn sowing and Masterpiece for spring.

Broccoli
Rudolf for an early crop followed by Red Arrow. The white varieties have a less attractive flavour in my opinion.

Brussels sprouts
Brigitte is a good early one and Doric will extend the season well.

Cabbage
For January try January King, although we are not too successful with them. Spring Hero starts our year and is succeeded by Greyhound for the early summer. Sherwood takes the late summer slot and we finish with Tundra.

Carrots
Early Nantes for early crops and for quick crops throughout the summer. Autumn King is the traditional storing carrot. Chantenay Red Cored for a change.

Cauliflower
All Year Round works quite well and Deakin is good for November cutting.

Celery and celariac
For self-blanching celery use Golden Self Blanching. For a trench type use Solid White. Celariac Giant Prague is the standard.

Chick Peas
From the kitchen cupboard.

Chicory
Witloof for forcing. For salads try Radicchio, Pain di Zuccerio and Wallone. The last is a frisee type sometimes categorized in catalogues as 'Endive'.

Chinese cabbage
Nikko F1.

Comfrey
Bocking #14.

Cornsalad
Verte de Cambrai.

Cress
Cressida.

Cucumber
The only one we grow from seed is Natsuhikari. Otherwise we buy plants. Try any of the F1 hybrids.

French Beans
Boston is serving us well and Cobra when we want a climbing one.

Globe Artichokes
Best not from seed as they don't always come 'true'. Try Concerto F1 bought as plants.

Horseradish
As far as I know there is only one variety and that is the same as the wild one.

Jerusalem Artichokes
Fuseau is a smoother variety which is easier to prepare for the table. Otherwise, use any you can get.

Kohl Rabi
We like Logo.

Kale
Redbor grows well for us. Try Thousand Head if livestock is your main consumer (the flavour is less good but it bulks up well).

Lettuce
The list of possibles is very long and we keep experimenting. However, you must never be without Little Gem. Our other staple is Brunia but we have only ever found that in France.

Lucerne
Only one variety as far as I'm aware.

Marrow family
Green Bush is fine.

Mustard
Only one variety for green manure – just 'mustard'. Some oriental types are also available to grow for salads.

Onion family
Although there are many varieties of Garlic available we usually just plant cloves from any good bulbs. Early Wight is popular. For leeks, Musselburgh is good – currently we use Toledo. Sturon is our standard onion variety from sets – it keeps well. Radar is a reliable autumn planted variety. Shallots can successfully be grown from those bought to eat, especially if they have kept well. Otherwise try Golden Gourmet.

Parsnips
Tender and True, Countess and Gladiator have all served us well.

Peas
Feltham First is a reliable early pea and Hurst Green Shaft is really good for a slightly later crop.

Potatoes
First early potatoes – the best flavour are Epicure but they are at their best for a very short season. Try Rocket instead it's nearly as nice Accent has been good too. For second earlies Nadine takes some beating – will store quite well. Maincrop try Stemster (Red) Pink Fir Apple (Salad potato).

Radish
Dix Huit Jours needs to be brought home from your French holidays. French Breakfast is OK and Cherry Belle another good one. For winter radish, use China Rose.

Rhubarb
I've never bought any named varieties.

Runner Beans
White Lady is a nice white flowered variety but I still prefer Scarlet Emperor

Spinach and variants
New Zealand works best in dry conditions and Winter Giant is the standard. For Swiss Chard, take an Italian holiday. We bought 'Bietola da coste verde a costa larga argentata 2' in Sardinia and it is vastly better than any others we have grown. However, if you can't get that Swiss Chard appears as a variety of Leaf Beet in the British catalogues.

Salsify
Any – all pretty much the same.

Sweet Corn
Earlybird is good. Add Sweet Nugget for a longer season.

Tares
Whatever you can get.

Tomato
Pink Brandy Wine, a beefsteak type, is the best flavour and the hardest to grow. Gardeners' Delight is a good cherry type. Alicante is a good, more conventional type.

Turnip and swede
Golden Ball and Snowball are both old favourite turnips. For swede try Marian.

Winter Purslane
One variety only.

Glossary

Ark A movable pen for poultry or other small livestock. It is usually of light construction and it may have a couple of wheels at one end to enable it to be moved easily.

Biological control A method of controlling pests (including insects, caterpillars, mites and plant diseases) that relies on the introduction of predators, parasites, diseases or other natural mechanisms specific to the targeted pest.

BSE (Bovine spongiform encephalopathy) Commonly known as mad cow disease. It is a disease of cattle that causes a spongy degeneration of the brain and spinal cord

Cordon A method of training and pruning fruit trees/bushes to produce a single fruit-bearing stem, often growing at an angle.

Colostrum Milk produced in the first few days after giving birth that is essential for introducing disease resistance and extra vitamins and minerals to the offspring.

Curd The white part of cauliflower.

DEFRA Department for Food, the Environment, Farming and Rural Affairs.

E-coli A bacterium that is commonly found in the lower intestine. Most strains are harmless, but some can cause serious food poisoning in humans.

Espalier The result of training (fruit) trees and bushes through pruning in order to create formal two-dimensional patterns by the branches, usually in order to train them against a wall or fence.

Factory farming Is the practice of raising livestock in confinement at a high stocking density.

Feed hopper A container which holds a large volume of feed with access for the livestock to eat from the bottom.

GM crops Genetically modified crops.

Hybrid vigour Increased performance gained by crossing two distinct varieties of plants or animals together (eg. faster growth rates, larger plants, more eggs).

Humus Degraded organic material in soil.

Kindle, to A term used for rabbits when they give birth. A pregnant doe is also said to be 'in kindle'.

Mulch A protective layer placed over the soil to suppress weed growth and/or feed the plants, for example compost, bark, manure or woven 'landscaping' material.

Paunch, to Remove guts after slaughter.

Perennial A plant that lives for more than two years.

Pollinator A compatible plant that is a source of pollen to allow fruits to form on another plant.

Polytunnel A structure made of polythene on a metal frame used to provide a sheltered growing environment.

Propagate To reproduce plants by seeds, cuttings, grafting or other methods.

Rootball The clump of roots on an established plant.

Rootstock A plant whose root system is used for grafting a bud or scion (small piece) from another plant. The use of rootstocks is common with fruit trees.

Salmonella Bacteria which cause illnesses in humans and many animals generally described as food poisoning.

Scrapie A disease of sheep that causes a spongy degeneration of the brain and spinal cord similar to BSE in cattle.

Spit The amount of earth/turf that is turned by a spade.

Spongiform encephalopathy see **BSE**.

Taproot A straight tapering plant root that grows vertically downward.

Index